Tourism: Management of Facilities

Anthea Rogers and Judy Slinn

M&E

THE M&E HANDBOOK SERIES

PITMAN PUBLISHING
128 Long Acre, London WC2E 9AN

A Division of Longman Group UK Limited

© Longman Group UK Limited 1993

First published in Great Britain 1993
Reprinted 1993

British Library Cataloguing in Publication Data
A catalogue entry for this book is available from the British Library.

ISBN 0-7121-2043-2

Printed and bound in Singapore

Contents

Preface

This handbook has been designed and written for all managers in the tourism industry, current and aspiring. It focuses on the key skills, knowledge and competences required to manage effectively in this service industry. It should provide a framework for students on undergraduate and diploma courses. The text uses examples and cases to illustrate the application of management concepts and their relevance to real world situations. Few texts have been written on management in the tourist industry and those that are available have tended to concentrate on the hotel and catering sector. We have therefore deliberately avoided using examples from that sector and looked elsewhere for illustrations and cases. As well as stressing the practical aspects of management and the environmental concepts, emphasis is placed on appraising and evaluating performance in line with the recent recommendations of two National Economic Development Council (NEDC) reports (*Developing managers for tourism* and *UK tourism – Competing for Growth*).

The progress tests at the end of each chapter will allow readers to test their understanding at each stage. Although they are presented in separate categories for students and managers, there are overlaps and both groups of readers would benefit from attempting questions in each sector.

The writing reflects our experience of teaching management at undergraduate level and we are grateful to past students whose comments and perceptions have enlightened our approach. Our thanks also to the industry, particularly to Alan Smith, John Wheale, Peter Haylings and Julia Watson who contributed quotations we have used.

Special thanks to Emma Coles of the School of Business at Oxford Brookes University who produced the diagrams.

H. Anthea Rogers
Judy Slinn

Part one

The manager's job in the tourism industry

Introduction to part one

The external environment

An understanding of the external environment in which any organization operates and the constraints and opportunities this affords is an essential prerequisite to appreciating the challenges that face management in general. Figure 1.1 summarizes the environment in which managers operate as they transform resources into the services required by customers. Chapter 1 examines the context of the manager's job before Chapter 2 looks in detail at the nature of managerial tasks.

1
The context of the job – understanding the industry

1. **Understanding the industry**

   Tourism is widely recognized as a fast growing and prosperous industry but building an accurate profile of it is difficult. Much of the statistical information that would usually be available in other more mature industries is only now becoming accessible and is still far from comprehensive. The collation and presentation of such information creates problems since many of the sectors such as transport and hotels which offer services to tourists do not do so exclusively.

2. **Environmental factors**

   Enterprises in the tourism industry transform resources – land, labour and capital – into the end product of the industry, in this case represented by services at attractions and facilities. All parts of this process, from the availability of the resources to the demand for the services will be influenced by factors in the environment which can be classified under six headings: ecological, legal, technical, economic, social and political (*see* Figure 1.1). This categorization is also useful for identifying the key factors in the environment which have influenced the growth of the industry so far and are likely to do so in the future.

   Demographic trends and changes have been reinforced by increasing affluence evidenced by rising real incomes and combined with increased leisure and recreational time.

   Technological innovation has offered greater mobility and access to travel; the development of the air transport industry over the past 40 years is a good example of such a trend. The growth of the tourism industry reflects both the desire to travel for educational, recreational and cultural reasons and the development of the means to do so.

   The industry has been under-researched until recently and environmental analysis has been piecemeal. To some extent it is a reflection of the difficulties involved in defining the tourism industry itself.

ENVIRONMENTAL FACTORS

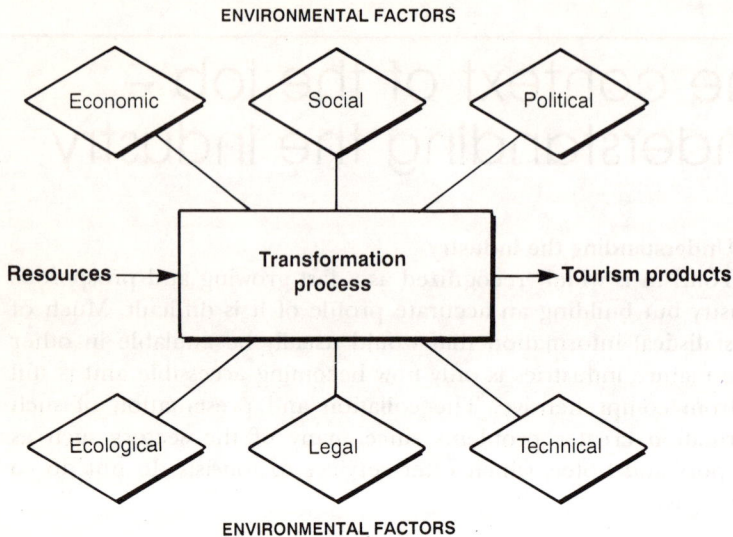

Figure 1.1 *The organization in the environment*

3.   Definition of the tourism industry

Agreement concerning the scope and nature of the industry has been difficult to secure and to date there is no universally acceptable definition. Most industries are usually defined from a supply side approach – in terms of the commodities they produce or the activities they undertake – but for tourism many of the existing definitions have focused on tourists and their motivation or tourism as a phenomenon and have, therefore, been almost exclusively demand based.

Within the UK the definition in most general use is that of the Tourism Society which is broad based and encompasses tourism and leisure activities:

> Tourism denotes the temporary short term movement of people to destinations outside the places where they normally live and work and their activities during their stay at these destinations . . . this definition includes domestic and international tourism comprising day visits as well as staying visits, for the following main purposes: holidays, leisure and recreation; business and conferences (Tourism Society Handbook)

This definition includes the activity undertaken and is more useful to our study of management of facilities since it permits us to examine the industry as a provider of 'tourism products', including leisure and recreation, that meet visitor needs. In 1991 an estimated 1.4 million people were employed in the industry, overseas earnings totalled £7.1 billion, and 16.6 million visitors came from abroad. (*Employment Gazette,* July 1992)

4. **Tourism products**
Any tourist visit requires a combination of services that may include all or a number of the following: attractions, transport, accommodation, refreshments (food and drink), shopping, entertainment, infrastructure and hopefully hospitality and a welcome. These component services may be provided by different organizations in the different sectors of the industry or on some occasions may be delivered by one organization as an integrated package. It is important for individual suppliers to recognize the role played in the total tourist product of their individual component; it may be the major draw that pulls tourists into the destination area or it may fulfil a subsidiary role in the bundle of services bought.
Knowing whether it is perceived as a primary or secondary attraction will have a substantial influence on management decisions, particularly in marketing.

5. **Components of the industry**
These are usually categorized under the following headings:

(a) attractions;
(b) facilities;
(b) infrastructure;
(d) transport;
(e) hospitality.

Although we can separate these components for analysis, the reality in practice is that there is considerable overlap and interaction and there are strong arguments from a management perspective to regroup the components under less arbitrary headings.

6. **Attractions**
These may be natural or man-made and they usually provide the initial stimulus or motivation for the visit. They include natural features of the landscape such as mountains, lakes and beaches to be found in areas considered to be of outstanding scenic beauty

such as the Lake District, the Northumberland Coast, the lochs and glens of Scotland and the mountains of Wales; unique physical phenomena such as the Niagara Falls or the Grand Canyon in the USA; climates favourable to the individual tourist's taste, whether it is sun in which to bask or adequate quantities of snow for the skier.

Man-made attractions range from archaeological remains from pre-tourism eras such as the Aztec tombs in Mexico, pyramids in Egypt, Roman baths in Europe and the striking architecture of the Greeks or other civilizations to the purpose-built tourist attractions of the twentieth century such as the theme parks of Disneyland or Alton Towers, the heritage and maritime centres and events such as garden festivals.

There were estimated to be around 5500 tourist attractions registered with the ETB/BTA (English Tourist Board/British Tourist Authority) in 1990. They were categorized in five groups under the headings: *Historic buildings* (1347), *Gardens* (305), *Museums and art galleries* (1547), *Wildlife attractions* (236) and *Other attractions*. In some cases the categorization is rather arbitrary. The main categories under *Other attractions* are country parks (181), farms (138), leisure parks (53), steam railways (90), visitor centres (147) and workplaces open to the public (294).

The 1991 Visitor Attraction Survey undertaken by the BTA revealed the following attendance for the overall top five attractions charging admissions:

1. Madame Tussauds 2,248,956; 2. Alton Towers 1,968,000; 3. Tower of London 1,923,520; 4. Natural History Museum 1, 571, 681; 5. St Paul's Cathedral 1,500,000.

Top of the list for *Historic buildings* was the Tower of London; in *Gardens*, Tropical World, Leeds, headed the table with 1,062,654 followed closely by Hampton Court with 1,000,000; in *Museums and art galleries*, the British Museum had over 5 million visitors; for the *Wildlife attractions* category London Zoo had 1.1 million and Windsor Safari Park 899,076. Under *Other attractions*, Blackpool Pleasure Beach topped all attendances with 6.5 million followed by the Palace Pier, Brighton, with 3.5 million.

Charges for entry are made at approximately 64 per cent of attractions; of these 50 per cent charge less than £2 per entry; estimates of total visitor expenditure vary but a realistic figure appears to be in the region of £800 milllion. The size of attractions varies considerably: the smallest attractions receiving less than 1000 visitors per annum account for 10 per cent of all attractions; 24 per cent of the numerical distribution of attractions attract over 50,000 visitors per year; 7 per cent attract 200,000 visitors which is 60 per cent of all estimated visits. There are 110 attractions receiving more than 500,000 visitors a year.

7. Facilities

These are needed to enhance the enjoyment from attractions. They include accommodation, ranging from luxury hotels to camp and caravan sites; food and beverage units that may offer superb cuisine or fast food snacks at realistic prices; shopping, increasingly an important part of tourist activity, which may be provided in the shape of speciality complexes with sophisticated or speciality themes or at small craft centres. Visitor centres that provide information or booking services may also fall into this category and some have been developed into attractions in their own right, for example National Trust Centres in Scotland.

8. Infrastructure

Tourist destinations, whether large or small require the basic necessities that infrastructure supplies – water, sewerage treatment and disposal, health care and security – although the level of sophistication required will vary. Transport and communications, such as roads for example, can be categorized as infrastructure but are more usually given special status as a component in their own right.

9. Transport

Travel is implicit in tourism and it may entail transport by air, sea, rail or road. The provision of communication networks at least at a basic level is a prerequisite for tourist development. Large-scale tourist movements will require more sophisticated passenger-handling facilities such as airport or rail terminals and the operational effectiveness of these will have a direct influence on the perceived quality of the total product. Managerial expertise and competence have to be at a high level if the exacting and high-quality expectations of modern tourists are to be satisfactorily met.

10. Hospitality

The welcome given to visitors at a specific attraction or facility enhances or detracts from the experience and influences the overall impression the tourist takes away. Host interaction is seen as an increasingly important determinant of tourist choice: the hospitality extended in all the component sectors of the tourism industry is influential in determining the reputation of that sector and the individual attraction or facility within it. Good reputations take time and effort to establish and to maintain; they can be lost too or at least seriously damaged as a result of a casual uncontrolled encounter, particularly if it attracts adverse publicity.

11. Interrelationships

The component categories discussed in 5–10 above are not mutually exclusive and attractions or facilities may fall into two or even more categories. Some examples will illustrate:

(a) Gleneagles Hotel may be regarded as a facility for the benefit of visitors to Scotland but to many guests using its facilities it is an attraction in its own right because of its ambience, reputation and the wide range of leisure opportunities that it can offer.

(b) Infrastructure developments built to provide water and generate electricity have become tourist attractions in themselves both in the UK, where this is the case with the Kielder dam in Northumberland and the Dinorwic pump storage scheme in North Wales, and overseas, for example the Kariba dam on the Zambia/Zimbabwe border.

(c) Within areas of outstanding natural beauty such as the National Parks the scenery is the prime attraction. However, facilities are also needed to maximize the enjoyment of visitors. These may range from outlets at the edge of wilderness areas supplying guidebooks and maps, to carefully signposted camping or information centres which are more centrally located and staffed by wardens. In more accessible parks, facilities may include an attractively designed and well managed visitor centre offering food and drink and interpretation through the use of exhibitions and videos. Such a centre and the facilities it supplies can itself become a major man-made attraction within the park.

(d) 'The little trains of Wales', the narrow steam gauge railways, attract a wide range of international visitors, including railway buffs, who also provide a core of visitors to other resuscitated railways. In Wales the railways provide transport to scenic areas and other facilities – food, beverages and shopping – in their station complexes. In Scotland the railways now run inclusive and up-market tours that also provide an accommodation component.

It is therefore dangerous to regard the components as exclusive categories and it must be accepted that many operators find themselves astride more than one tourism defined category.

Facilities may not be used exclusively by tourists, for example, sports and leisure complexes built principally for the use of local residents will enhance the attraction of an area to tourists, while successful tourist attractions will also enjoy repeat visits from local residents. For this reason in the rest of this text the terms 'attractions' and 'facilities' are used interchangeably because the managerial tasks in airport terminals, theme parks, heritage centres or accommodation units share common features through the service element that is implicit in their provision.

The most appropriate and widely accepted definition of a tourist attraction is that given in 1989 by the Scottish Tourist Board:

> a permanently established excursion destination, a primary purpose of which is to allow public access for entertainment interest or education rather than being principally a retail outlet or venue for sports, theatrical or film performances. Open to the public without prior booking for a published period per year and attracting tourist visitors as well as local residents

A recent survey by BMRB (British Market Research Bureau) conducted for LR (Leisure Research) Consultants concluded that 73 per cent of UK adults visit some kind of attraction each year, museums and historic buildings being the most popular followed by theme parks and zoos.

Example : Leisure Day Visits Survey _____

In view of the increased recognition of the importance of day trips and leisure visits to tourist attractions, a survey has been commenced on a regular basis by the Office of Population Censuses and Surveys (OPCS) on behalf of the Department of Employment, BTA and ETB. This concluded that for 1988/9 £5 billion was spent on day trips, (i.e. 20 per cent of total tourist expenditure or 50 per cent of domestic UK expenditure). Results from the Leisure Day Visits Survey 1988/89 were published in the *Employment Gazette* in May 1991. Its main conclusions show that during April 1988 to March 1989:

(a) Spending on day visits now exceeds 20 per cent of total tourism expenditure and is equivalent to nearly half of all domestic tourism expenditure;

(b) There were 630 million round trips in Great Britain of 3 hours or more and at least 20 miles, on which £5,212 million was spent;

(c) The most popular reason was for outdoor activities with 174 million trips (28 per cent); followed by visits to friends or relatives (144 million; 23 per cent), and to tourist attractions (82 million; 13 per cent);

(d)   The level of trip-taking was highest in summer and spring (177 and 176 million visits, or each 28 per cent of the total) followed by autumn (23 per cent) and winter (21 per cent);

(e)   The weekend was more popular overall (55 per cent of all trips) than weekdays, and Sunday was the most favoured day (30 per cent) followed by Saturday (25 per cent); Sunday was the favourite day to visit friends and relatives, attractions or to do outdoor activities;

(f)   Spending was highest on shopping trips, at £1,458 million (28 per cent of the total), outdoor activities (£598 million);

(g)   Average expenditure per person was highest on shopping trips (£22.80 each), followed by trips to public houses and restaurants (£12) and to theatres and bingo (£11.80);

(h)   The most visited tourist board regions were the Heart of England (70 million) and London (68 million);

(i)   The main type of place visited was an inland town or city (340 million visits), very much higher than the next most popular type of destination, a seaside town or village, beach, coast or estuary (103 million);

(j)   By far the majority of trips were made by car, van or motorcycle (86 per cent). A further 5 per cent were made by train or tube, 4 per cent by excursion coach, and 3 per cent by scheduled bus;

(k)   The average distance travelled per visit was 68.4 miles, nearly a quarter of all trips covering between 20 and 29 miles.

12. Features of services

The special characteristics involved in the provision of services differentiate the management task from that in manufacturing industries in a number of respects.

What are the special characteristics of services? Most of these stem from the fact that 'services are consumed in the process of their production' (Sasser, 1978).

As a result:

(a)   *The staff involved in providing the process are a part of the product –* their attitudes, behaviour and appearance contribute to consumers' perceptions. Unlike staff who are engaged in producing manufactured goods and are never seen by customers, the contribution of service staff in theme parks, museums, hotels or any facility is clearly observable to the public and the way that they present themselves is a crucial attribute of the service provided. The pivotal role of staff and their skills is a major challenge to management and the industry.

(b)   *The consumer is involved with the product –* some degree of customization always takes place. This may be at a superficial level, as for example in a fast food outlet where the customer helps in providing the service itself or it may be inextricably part of the product image as, for example, when a child relives the experience of a bygone educational era in the reconstructed school room of Wigan Pier, a heritage centre in Lancashire. This interactive process also means that the behaviour of one customer can have a spillover effect on the experience of another. Managerial discretion, therefore, will have to be exercised both as to the amount of involvement and as regards the procedures for managing visitor interactions.

(c) *There is no tangible product to carry home* – although the 'effects' of the experience may be taken away by the customer. Manufactured products are bought from sales assistants or by mail order and then used subsequently. If they prove unsatisfactory they may even be returned but tourism services are consumed in real time and only the memory of the experience is carried home. Shattered dreams are virtually impossible to replace if the reality did not meet the expectation. This intangibility also means that prior assessment of the experience is often impossible and evaluation can only be undertaken in retrospect. The degree of intangibility does however vary from sector to sector and in some areas can be manipulated to some extent by skilful marketing.

(d) *The process is non-storable and perishable.* Hotel rooms are regarded as the most perishable of products: the revenue from a bed unfilled is lost for ever. In the same way empty seats on aeroplanes or on theme park rides are spare capacity that can not be re-utilized. Because stocks cannot act as a buffer between the supply and demand gap, capacity planning and utilization are important management tasks.

(e) *The process is delivered at specific locations* – often in response to consumer preferences. Products that are storable and transportable may be produced wherever it is most convenient from a production angle and routed to the end user but facilities required by tourists have to be provided at locations convenient to the customer. These may well add additional costs to the process or create problems with staffing that are difficult to mitigate. This also makes demands on organizational structures since the need for multi-site operations often places an additional burden on management.

(f) *The surroundings of the delivery process are a feature of the service* – and affect consumers' perceptions. In manufacturing, the factory is designed to meet the functional requirements of the workforce and/or the product. In service industries, because the customer is involved in the process, the environment has to meet dual and often conflicting demands. For example, the most efficient lay-out in terms of achieving maximum throughput may not be the most aesthetically pleasing.

(g) *Most tourism services are rendered within discrete time periods* – (for example, a day excursion, a weekend break) and the demand patterns fluctuate through time, sometimes very inconsistently, which makes forecasting hazardous.

(h) *Tourism services are supplied directly to people not to inanimate objects.* Capacity planning and operational problems – scheduling, queuing and equipment failures – will therefore pose additional problems. People require to be treated with dignity and care; they cannot be stacked up until it is convenient for the operator to process their requests or until capacity is available. Sometimes they behave unpredictably and may even on occasions ignore safety procedures designed to protect them, so tact, diplomacy and interpersonal skills are required. This, together with the unpredictability of demand, causes problems in monitoring service levels and evaluating performance since traditional quality control measures cannot be employed.

The relevance of these service characteristics and their impact on management tasks will be reassessed as we proceed through the text.

13. Tourism suppliers

How are these services provided and who are the suppliers in the industry? Tourism facilities are provided by a wide variety of organizations and within each sector there are enterprises of all sizes and forms. Ownership is also varied with both the public and the private sector represented. Very few other industries have such an array and diversity of corporate forms.

Organizations can be categorized as *profit orientated* or *non-profit orientated.* The former are business organizations in that they exist to provide services at a profit, although making a profit may not be their sole aim. It should also be noted that organizations do not exist merely for a moment in time; they are not static but dynamic institutions needing to respond to internal and external pressures for their continuity. Their history and their future is, therefore, of relevance and though they are examined at one point in time they are always part of an evolutionary process. The type of corporate form employed at any one time should meet the needs of the organization at that time and for the foreseeable future. It will be influenced by such factors as the ease of formation, financial resources and requirements, taxation, legal constraints, management skills, motivation and personal objectives of those involved.

14. Types of corporate form
The options available are:

(a) *Sole proprietorship.* A form of business owned and controlled by one individual who receives all the profits, takes all the risks and bears all the losses if they occur. Sole proprietorships are the most numerically common form of businesses in services since they offer numerous *advantages:*

(*i*) They are easy to set up and dissolve.

(*ii*) They offer freedom to the owner in his objective setting and decision making. This independence is often highly prized by certain individuals who like being their own boss.

(*iii*) Profit retention acts as a strong incentive towards efficiency and profits can also be ploughed back into the business to allow expansion.

(*iv*) Flexibility and responsiveness to market conditions and consumer needs is expedited by the narrow decision making base and the limited need for consultation.

Disadvantages are also inherent in this type of corporate form:

(*i*) The unlimited liability may inhibit risk taking and lead to over cautious decision making.

(*ii*) The capital resources are limited to the owner's personal assets and may impede the required rate of expansion in a competitive world.

(*iii*) The management skills are limited to those of the owner and may prove inadequate as the business grows.

(*iv*) The business is vulnerable during times of illness and no continuity may be available in the event of death.

Examples of sole proprietorship abound in the tourism industry and can be found in the hotel and catering sector, in transport and in tourist attractions.

(b) *Partnership.* An association of two or more individuals who operate a business as co-owners under an agreement. If one of the partners takes no active role in the decision making he/she may be regarded as a sleeping partner and so have limited liability, otherwise the responsibility is shared equally. This is often a natural progression from a sole proprietorship if the additional partner can make a positive contribution in financial or managerial skills.

The *advantages* are:
(*i*) Ease of formation.
(*ii*) Flexibility.
(*iii*) Increased management skills and expertise.
(*iv*) Further financial resources.

The *disadvantages* are:
(*i*) Unlimited liability and legal responsibility for the actions of partners.
(*ii*) Immense interpersonal problems if the relationships between partners go sour or if consensus regarding strategies cannot be achieved; for example, if one partner wishes to expand the business and the other does not.
(*iii*) Long-term problems in continuity.
(*iv*) Problems of dissolution are invariably complex unless a new partner can be found.

(c) *Private limited company.* The business is owned by shareholders (of which there must be a minimum of two). It has a legal entity which is formalized when it is set up in the Memorandum and Articles of Association, which are legally required. It has limited liability but there are restraints on the conduct and behaviour of the directors who have to accept responsibility. Shares in the company can be bought and sold but not publicly. Access to capital is therefore dependent on the contacts available, since a Stock Exchange quotation cannot be sought. This type of corporate form has been the starting point for many large successful companies. It also offers security to family businesses in that it is not vulnerable to takeover by outsiders, and there are many companies that stay private for this reason.

Apart from the limited liability, privacy and security there are few merits in being a private company rather than a public limited company.

(d) *Public limited company.* The shareholders can issue shares to the public at large and so raise capital from numerous and diverse sources. A public company big enough to justify and strong enough to gain a Stock Exchange quotation has the added benefit of the increased liquidity that the Stock Exchange gives and is therefore able to borrow very substantial capital sums to finance investment.

The *advantages* of a public company are:
(*i*) Limited liability of shareholders.
(*ii*) Continuity over the long term and ease of ownership transfer.
(*iii*) Specialized management skills.
(*iv*) Large capital resources.
(*v*) Economies resulting from large scale operations.

Disadvantages may include:
(*i*) Expensive to set up.
(*ii*) Organizational problems resulting from size causing lack of flexibility.
(*iii*) Separation of ownership and control causing reduced or biased motivation.
(*iv*) Over expansion.

In this category is found the multinational company that has its registered office in one country but with substantial operations in foreign countries. There are also large companies only part of whose activities are in tourism: for example, Pearson, owners of such tourist attractions as Alton Towers and Madame Tussauds but also publishers and merchant bankers. Multinationals are an increasing phenomena in tourism and leisure and likely to become more so with Disney's new French theme park leading the way. In the hotel sector names such as Hilton, Hyatt and Intercontinental have internationally established corporate identities.

(e) *The franchise.* In a franchising agreement the franchisee agrees to pay the franchisor an amount – usually a flat fee plus royalties or commission – in return for the use of a national or international name and other help such as building plans and site selection where appropriate, production methods and management and accounting procedures in establishing and running the business. The cost, both initially and in the future, of buying into a franchise operation may be high but a successful franchise offers the person wanting to establish a business some reduction of the risk inherent in doing so. Franchising is common in the restaurant business and is becoming so in retailing. Among the hotel chains, Holiday Inn is an example. For large organizations, franchising may offer a way of providing more specialized facilities for the visitor without having to develop or take on more skilled staff and invest in equipment. At Thorpe Park, the theme park, water sport activities (with the exception of wind-surfing) have now been franchised to a specialist company who pay a rent for the use of the water and facilities.

15. Non profit seeking organizations

Non profit seeking organizations come in a variety of forms, many examples of which can be found in the tourism industry.

(a) *Charities and trusts.* The National Trust was incorporated as an independent organization with charitable status in 1907 to preserve buildings and land. Its income, derived from membership fees, from legacies, from visitors to its properties and from its commercial activities such as retailing, is used to acquire, preserve, manage and maintain in excess of 200 historic buildings, 544,000 acres of land and some 500 miles of coastline.

(b) *Cooperatives.* Enterprises owned and run by their managers and workers; this form is not as common in the UK as in mainland Europe. However, cooperative ventures, particularly for marketing or purchasing may be found. Best Western Hotels is one of the better known marketing hotel syndicates: Historic Houses enjoy joint marketing activities. Increasingly museums with common themes or in close geographic proximity offer joint promotions and engage in other joint marketing consortiums.

(c) *Local authorities.* Local authorities not only own leisure and sports complexes which are used by tourists as well as local inhabitants but also purpose built tourist attractions, such as Wigan Pier and the White Cliffs Experience at Dover; they also own a number of museums such as Cogges in West Oxfordshire. Local authorities, whether rural or municipal are increasingly involved, sometimes in joint ventures with commercial enterprises, in the development of tourism projects.

(d) *Public corporations.* Principally the form adopted by nationalized or state-owned enterprises in the past, such as, for example, the airline business British Airways, now after privatization a public company. Similarly the British Airports Authority was privatized in 1987. As far as the tourism industry is concerned the most significant public corporation left is British Rail, also scheduled for privatization.

(e) *Quangos.* Quangos are Quasi-Autonomous Non-Governmental Organizations such as the tourist boards and the Countryside Commission. The British Tourist Authority and the English, Scottish and Welsh Tourist Boards were established under the terms of the 1969 Development of Tourism Act which also allowed for the setting up of 'advisory committees'. The latter became the regional tourist boards. Funding of these derives partly from government via the ETB, partly from local authorities and partly from income generated by their own activities. The Sports Council is another body which is of significance to the industry because of its impact on leisure activities. Another quango is the Museums and Galleries Commission originally founded in 1931 but since 1982 playing a more active role as administrator of grants and advisory services.

16. Current management issues in the industry
One of the core problems in the industry is its comparative youth and the fast rate of development that has allowed little time for adjustment and consolidation. Some of the major challenges which face management in the industry which will be explored in this book are:

(a) Recognition of the fact that as a service industry the *calibre of staff* is a major determinant of success. Recruitment, staff development and training must, therefore, be given detailed attention. This will involve attitude changes on the part of management who will have to find a means of allowing discretionary flexibility while at the same time retaining control. The demographic trends which are forecast are likely to make staffing problems more acute. Julia Watson, MD of Career Concepts and ex-ETB training, has stated that

> if the tourism industry in the UK is to compete internationally in the 1990s, we must be able to offer high standards of service on a consistent basis. The people working in tourism are, therefore, the key to its future success. First class training is required to provide both new entrants and existing staff with the knowledge, skills and attitudes required to satisfy visitor expectations.

This last point is linked to the question of consumer tastes.

(b) *Changing consumer tastes*, particularly the demand for high quality of both the product and its presentation, will inevitably require a high level of service and investment. The increasing internationalization of consumer tastes will place new demands on managers to meet them while maintaining individual character. Alan Smith, Operations Director for Heritage Projects (Management) Ltd, responding to a query in this area, stated that 'at the individual level, the greatest challenge is simple; making every visitor feel that they are "special".'
(c) Ensuring the availability of long-term *capital* for the development of the industry by making it attractive to the City and other investors.

(d) Comprehending the implications of 1992 and the repercussions that the creation of a *single market* will have on the competitive environment in which firms operate for both customers and staff.

(e) Finding ways of *motivating staff* at the facility level to adopt the right attitudes and acquire the necessary skills in order to provide high quality service. John Wheale, personnel manager at BTA, commented:

> the tourism industry must learn to appreciate that its most important resource is its people, to treat this resource with respect, and to find new and innovative ways to unleash people's ability and talents within the organizational framework . . . there needs to be a fundamental rethink by every organization to use its people resource more effectively and efficiently, not only at the top of the organization but in every aspect of the work environment.

(f) Acting in a *socially responsible* way towards the environment and society. In particular, at an operational level managers must be aware of the impact of their attraction on the host community. Alan Smith again:

> the biggest problem facing tourism today is finding the correct balance between exploitation and conservation of our heritage. This applies as much to the trails and paths across the Lake District, as it does to our world class monuments like Stonehenge. If we are not careful, we may irreparably harm the very fabric that attracts millions of visitors to Britain.

On the positive side organizations may offer employment opportunities to local labour and increase local income but at the same time they may play a part in creating congestion, leading to cultural, aesthetic and environmental degradation. The negative effects may well be in direct proportion to the success of the attraction. The significance of the issue of sustainable tourism, to which the ETB's Tourism and the Environment Task Force addressed itself in its report *Tourism and the environment – Maintaining the balance*, published in May 1991, is likely to increase in the coming years.

Progress test 1

For students

S1. What are the main problems encountered when undertaking external environmental analysis in the industry? **(1, 2)**

S2. What is meant by referring to tourism products as a 'bundle of services'? Identify the components. **(4, 5)**

S3. Review the tourism attractions of your home or college area: under how many different headings could they be classified? **(6)**

S4. Identify the infrastructure facilities used by tourists in your area. Analyze critically the extent to which they meet tourist needs. **(8, 9, 10)**

S5. What is meant by the 'intangibility' of services? Is this an advantage or a drawback for marketing purposes? **(12)**

S6. Why is location so important to tourism service providers? **(12)**

S7. How do tourism enterprises deal with fluctuating demand levels? Illustrate your answer with examples. **(12)**

S8. List the variety of corporate forms found in the tourism industry. Select examples from your locality to illustrate these. **(14)**

S9. Set out the reasons why franchising has become so popular in the UK. Select a few examples to illustrate your answer. **(14)**

S10. Local authorities and other public sector organizations are playing an increasingly important role in UK tourism. Why? **(14, 15)**

S11. Why do managers in the industry regard staffing as one of the major challenges facing the industry today. **(16)**

S12. Why was the tourism task force set up in 1990? What is the significance of their recommendations for managerial decision-making in the 1990s? **(16)**

For managers and practitioners

M1. How often does your organization undertake an analysis of the external environment in which it operates? What are the main problems encountered and how are they dealt with? **(1, 2)**

M2. Does your organization provide a primary or a secondary component within the tourism industry? How might this affect the marketing strategy used? **(4)**

M3. How much emphasis is given to 'welcome' aspects of hospitality in your facility? **(10)**

M4. To what extent do you consider staff attitudes affect consumers' perceptions of the service you offer? **(10, 12)**

M5. Assess the degree of customerization and customer involvement in your 'tourism product'. **(12)**

M6. What proportion of your service involves direct contact between staff and customers? What are the implications of this? **(12)**

M7. Does the demand from your customers fluctuate? How variable is it? What action is taken to allow for this? **(12)**

M8. Under what type of corporate form could your organization be classified? What are the major merits and drawbacks from an organizational perspective? **(14)**

M9. Could the activity of your organization be satisfactorily franchised? Give reasons for your answer. **(14)**

M10. Is your organization publicly or privately owned? What might be the effect on its overall policy if the form of ownership was altered from private to public or vice versa? **(15)**

M11. Interview one of the managers (or the owner) of your organization, asking him/her what he/she sees as the major challenge facing management in the tourism industry. **(16)**

M12. What are the implications for your organization of the recommendations made by the task force report *Tourism and the environment – Maintaining the Balance* in May 1991. **(16)**

2
The manager's job

1. The role of a manager

The manager's job is central to the transformation process in which all organizations are involved. We have already examined how organizations will vary in activity, scope, size and ownership and emphasized how these will influence their objectives and behaviour. We shall look at organizational objectives more closely in the next chapter but it should be noted at this stage that no organization, whether in the private or the public sector, can provide a service regardless of price. The objective of providing the service for the tourist will, therefore, be defined within the context of either making a profit for the shareholders or the owner or within a cost constraint.

2. What does a manager do?

Looking more closely at what managers actually *do* as agents of the transformation process we can adopt a number of approaches that shed light on the activity. Management may be defined in a general way as getting things done through people and more specifically by defining managerial functions or by looking at the roles managers play.

3. The manager's time

First let us look at what activities might occupy a manager's time on a typical day. The following schedule (Figure 2.1) has been constructed on the basis of a survey of managers from the tourism industry to give some indication of the different aspects of the operation with which a manager may be concerned.

4. Analyzing the day

The manager's day described in Figure 2.1 exhibits a number of characteristics confirmed by research and observation of managers in a wide spectrum of organizations. The first of these is that at any level a manager's job contains variety, fragmentation and frequent interruptions. The contacts with many people at

8.15	deals with post and takes a number of phone calls
8.30	meeting with maintenance manager
9.00	brief tour of facility to check all is well; while doing so discusses with a member of staff the latter's personal problems
9.30	annual appraisal interview with operations manager
10.30	dictates letters, returns phone calls received in previous hour
11.00	receives group of overseas visitors for coffee and introduces them to senior staff who will be looking after them
11.30	unscheduled meeting with accountant to discuss problems which have arisen
11.45	meeting, originally scheduled for 11.30, with personnel manager to discuss staffing requirements for peak holiday season and recruitment of extra casual staff.
12.30	lunch with overseas visitors until 2.00
2.00	dictates letters, makes phone calls
2.30	meeting with marketing manager to agree new advertising campaign
3.00	begins review of previous month's operations and visitor numbers for draft regular report for Head Office, interrupted by several telephone calls, arranges visit to Head Office later in the week, sees off overseas visitors
3.45	unscheduled problem with catering supplies
4.15	starts work on drafting next year's budget, interrupted by telephone calls, signing letters, checking memos
5.00	leaves to attend trade association conference starting at 6pm

Figure 2.1 *A typical day in the life of a manager of a tourist facility*

different levels inside and outside the organization are carried on through the use of many different modes of communication: paper, meetings and the telephone. However much the manager schedules his day, unanticipated problems arise, many of which require his action and authority to resolve, often immediately. Most managers find it difficult to spend time alone and make space for reflection but at the same time their jobs require them not only to keep the operation running as efficiently as possible in the present, but also to plan for the future.

5. Managerial work patterns

The pattern of managerial work described above was further substantiated by evidence from a study of 15 general managers carried out by Kotter (1982). A similar study of nine restaurant managers found the following pattern overall:

unscheduled meetings	35%
scheduled meetings	29%
desk sessions	17%
telephone calls	13%
tours	6%
Total	100%

(Ferguson and Berger, 1984)

6. Fayol's categorization of management

The first attempts to categorize managerial activities did so from a *functional* aspect. Henri Fayol (1841–1925), a French engineer, suggested that there were eight basic functions with which managers in any organization, large or small, were concerned (Fayol, 1949):

(a) determining and deciding objectives
(b) forecasting
(c) planning
(d) organizing
(e) directing
(f) co-ordinating
(g) controlling
(h) communicating.

7. A framework for analysis

These still provide a framework for analyzing managerial jobs in broad terms. All the activities can be found in the typical manager's day. The framework aids identification of the skills required to do the job, but it must be recognized that managerial tasks often fall across more than one category and that the eight functions will be distributed differently, depending on the specific nature of the job and the level of the manager. Senior managers are, or should be, more concerned with planning and deciding objectives than with day to day organizing.

8. Drucker's functions of management

The functions of management have been redefined by Peter Drucker into five basic operations in the following terms:

(a) setting objectives
(b) organizing
(c) motivating and communicating

(d) measuring performance
(e) developing people.

9. Interpersonal relations

There is an increasing knowledge now available about the way in which people behave and interact within organizations. The classical school of management theorists, which includes Fayol, assumes a simplicity and rationality of behaviour that later studies, from Elton Mayo onwards (whose work is known as the behavioural school), have shown does not exist (Mayo 1933). The behaviour of managers and workers alike is now known to be complex and sometimes irrational.

10. Understanding the job

All managers to a greater or lesser extent plan, organize, motivate and control. These are, however, very broad and general definitions, which may not help the individual manager seeking to understand his job or the outsider looking at it. The need to know more about the manager's job, in order to recruit people with the essential qualities and skills and to provide them with the necessary training (*see* Example) led to further empirical research about how managers actually spent their time and with whom. In other industries this is now well established.

Example ———————————————————————————————————

On being asked about the issues and problems facing tourist attraction managers, Peter Haylings, MD at Wookey Hole Caves, stated that there was one area where particular attention will have to be paid in the future; that is, the supply of trained junior staff suitable for developing as managers. The tourist attraction area of tourism is by its very nature very unstructured, being made up of many small entrepreneurial businesses which tend to be very different to each other. Unlike the hotel and travel industries it is difficult to establish a clear career path with appropriate qualifications. Many entering the industry as managers come with other skills and professional qualifications and very few have tourism qualifications, though some acquire these later.

These issues are now being addressed by the industry but there is a need to focus on the skills and competences that are needed for effective management.

———————————————————————————————————

11. Henry Mintzberg

Henry Mintzberg observed managers at work over a period of time and from his study suggested that managerial work could be described in terms of the *roles* that managers are required to play. He identified ten roles which he then grouped into three linked categories (Mintzberg 1973):

(1) *Interpersonal roles* describe the relations the manager has with other people inside and outside the organization. They are:

(a) figurehead
(b) leader
(c) liaison.

(2) *Informational roles* cover the collection and communication of information by the manager. They are:

(d) monitor
(e) disseminator
(f) spokesperson.

(3) *Decisional roles* result from the information and insights gained from the previous two categories and how the manager makes decisions:

(g) entrepreneur
(h) disturbance handler
(i) resource allocator
(j) negotiator.

12. Identification of Mintzberg's ten roles

Mintzberg argues that the ten roles are common to all managerial jobs although in practice one role often overlaps with another.

13. Managerial demands and constraints

Another approach to analyzing the managerial job, again based on empirical research exploring the nature of managerial activity and contacts, has been suggested by Rosemary Stewart (1976). Managerial activities and tasks, she argues, are carried out and jobs are shaped by a combination of demands, constraints and choices. Every job carries some responsibilities, some activities which must be performed to meet targets and criteria set. The extent to which the individual manager is constrained by, for example, organizational policies and procedures will vary from one organization to another and sometimes from one level within the organization to another. Given the demands and the constraints, most jobs will give the manager an area of choice about what he does and how he does it. Analyzing the job from this perspective allows the manager himself, as well as other observers, to understand more about his work and the way he does it.

14. Managerial skills

Approaching the problem from a different angle, we can look at the nature of the tasks required of managers and the skills needed to perform those tasks. There is a general consensus that managers need three broad categories of skills: *technical, human* and *conceptual.* In recent years the attempt made by a number of large organizations and approved by the Management Charter Initiative to use a competency-based system for performance appraisal (*see* Chapter 12) has broken these three broad categories into more specific skills which also throw more light on the nature of the managerial task.

15. Common skills in management

A competency, or core skill as some companies denote them, has been defined as an observable skill or ability to complete a managerial task successfully. Some companies also describe them as dimensions of managerial behaviour. Without, at this stage, examining in detail the processes used for identifying competences, what is significant is the marked similarity between the groups or clusters of skills recognized by a number of different companies in diverse industrial and service sectors. This suggests that, whatever the criticisms that can and should be made of the use of a competency-based system in appraisal, the skills do provide a way of distinguishing both the commonalty and the differences of management jobs.

16. Managerial performance factors

Henley Management College has compiled a list of twelve 'independent performance factors' or 'supra competences', divided into four groups which have a wide acceptance as key behaviours:

(1) *Intellectual*
(a) strategic perspective
(b) analysis and judgment
(c) planning and organizing.

(2) *Interpersonal*
(d) managing staff
(e) persuasiveness
(f) assertiveness and decisiveness
(g) interpersonal sensitivity
(h) oral communication.

(3) *Adaptability*
(i) adaptability and resilience.

(4) *Results-orientation*
(j) energy and initiative
(k) achievement-motivation
(l) business sense.

Readers will note the reappearance of key characteristics which have already appeared in the lists of functions and roles earlier in this chapter.

17. Quinn's key management roles
The most recent attempt to synthesize comprehensively the concepts of roles and competences comes from R. E. Quinn *et al.* (1990) who have identified eight major management roles with three key competences for each, as follows:

(1) *Director role*
(a) taking initiative
(b) goal setting
(c) delegating effectively.

(2) *Producer role*
(a) personal productivity and motivation
(b) motivating others
(c) time and stress management.

(3) *Coordinator role*
(a) planning
(b) organizing and designing
(c) controlling.

(4) *Monitor role*
(a) reducing information overload
(b) analyzing information critically
(c) presenting information: writing effectively.

(5) *Mentor role*
(a) understanding yourself and others
(b) interpersonal communication
(c) developing subordinates.

(6) *Facilitator role*
(a) team building
(b) participative decision making
(c) conflict management.

(7) *Innovator role*
(a) living with change
(b) creative thinking
(c) managing change.

(8) *Broker role*
(a) building and maintaining a power base
(b) negotiating agreement and commitment
(c) presenting ideas.

18. Where does all this take us?

Theoretical frameworks and models of the managerial job, its tasks and responsibilities and the skills it requires are useful in aiding our understanding of the processes involved. A common feature of all managerial jobs is that managers are decision makers: they transform resources to meet customer needs. The quality of the decisions taken will directly influence the performance of the organization. The nature and difficulty of the decisions will vary: some will be routine others will be unique.

19. Decision making

Routine decisions are programmable in the sense that they are taken in a relatively stable environment and so have a predictable outcome. Rules and regulations based on definite criteria can be established from previous experiential learning. In many organizations stock control, scheduling operations and staff activity would be typical examples of this type of decision making. It is usually designated as tasks to be performed within a given agenda, with limited discretionary powers, by lower or middle management. It is seen as the training ground for advancement to more senior positions where *unique decisions* that are non-programmable have to be made. These unique decisions are complex, elusive and invariably have uncertain outcomes since they are taken in a dynamic context. The specification of the agenda to be considered and the information base to be used requires judgement, skill and experience. Location, product selection, research and development are examples of decisions taken by and preoccupying top management because of their strategic implications.

20. The managerial task

Taken together the various approaches indicate that management is an *integrative* task, bringing together functions, roles and competences to achieve the objectives of the organization. Managers are agents of the transformation process which takes the inputs to the system and transforms them into the outputs, for our purposes those required in the tourism industry. While ensuring this is done in the most effective and efficient way possible, managers must also be aware that the system in which they work is not closed; it operates in a rapidly changing environment to which they and the business must respond. These strategic issues are the concern of the next chapter.

Progress test 2

For students

S1. Why is the transformation process of any tourist attraction dependent on the manager? **(1)**

S2. Interview the manager of a local tourist attraction and ask him/her to describe a typical day. Now compare this with our example and highlight any differences. How could these be explained? **(3)**

S3. How did Fayol categorize managerial activities? **(6)**

S4. What are the essential differences between Fayol's and Drucker's lists regarding management functions? **(6, 7)**

S5. Review the activities that your interview with the manager revealed and in so far as you are able identify the technical, conceptual and human skills that would be needed. **(14)**

S6. Review Quinn's key management roles and apply this to your selected manager. **(17)**

S7. Distinguish between routine and unique decisions. **(19)**

For managers and practitioners

M1. What is your role in the transformation process undertaken by your organization? **(1)**

M2. Set out in terms of time expended what is a typical day for you. Compare this with the examples in the text. **(4)**

M3. Do the functional aspects of management as depicted by Fayol match your activity patterns? **(6)**

M4. Take a cross sample of other managers in your organization and compare their activities, time allocations and schedules. Analyze the differences in terms of the nature of their work, their seniority or other relevant factors that you can identify. **(14)**

M5. To what extent do you agree with the statements made by Peter Haylings. Does your organization recognize the skills and training that are needed by managers in the industry. **(10)**

M6. Monitor your role within the organization. What are the core skills that you use frequently? Of the categories explored in the text which ones are the most appropriate for your activities? **(16, 17)**

M7. What type of decision making are you primarily involved in? **(18, 19)**

M8. Would you define your role as integrative; or is it clearly defined? **(20)**

Part two

Working in organizations

Introduction to part two

This part reviews the essential activities that are undertaken by organizations as they set goals and objectives, and design the structures that will enable goals to be achieved. Finally, it examines the specific tasks and jobs involved. These chapters are intended to provide an internal perspective on how organizations in the industry operate.

3
Setting objectives

1. **Determining the framework**
    We have noted in the last chapter that all organizations have
    objectives or goals (the two are used synonymously) which provide a
    framework of purpose for the organization, however large or small.
    The organization itself cannot have objectives although in
    identifying its major purpose we often speak as though it has.
    Objectives are frequently multiple, framed by the stakeholders' (i.e
    shareholders, employees, etc.) interests: they may include
    profitability in terms of the rate of return on capital invested;
    growth as measured by asset value, turnover or market share;
    autonomy and independence for the owner or managers; prestige
    and/or power for owners; social responsibility towards consumers,
    society and/or the physical environment. In hard times the focus
    may be on survival and the continuity of the business.

2. **Defining a mission statement**
    Identifying and articulating the organization's purpose in
    general terms is often done in a *mission statement*. Cynics have
    described these as a set of platitudes for legitimizing the
    organization, but organizations both large and small find that they
    serve a number of purposes.

    Example : BAA mission statement _____

    BAA is the world's leading international airport group. We own eight UK
    airports accounting in total for some 70% of UK passenger traffic and 85%
    of air cargo.
    We aim to maintain world leadership by placing the highest priority on
    safety and security . . . continuously improving quality of service and
    value for money . . . continuously improving our productivity . . .
    being 'easy to do business with' . . . ensuring our staff are well
    motivated and informed . . . and adopting an environmentally sensitive
    approach to all our developments. By achieving these goals we shall
    succeed in developing our core airport and related business – and
    enhancing the value of our shareholders' investments. (BAA *Annual Report
    and Accounts*)

3. **The value of a mission statement**

The purpose of such a mission statement is to clarify for all interested parties (stakeholders):

(a) what the organization is and the business it is in;
(b) where it is going in the short term and in the long term;
(c) how it intends to get there.

Some writers insist that a mission statement should include an element of 'vision', to excite and inspire its stakeholders, emphasizing the direction the senior managers have chosen to go in order to achieve more than mere survival. They also argue that, to be of significance, the statement should reflect the corporate value system (philosophy or culture) and indicate how its business is differentiated from that of its competitors.

4. **The relevance of a mission statement**

Not all mission statements answer all these demands but most try to set out the where, why and how questions for the organization, whether it is profit making or non-profit making. In large organizations particularly a mission statement can serve an integrative function in bringing together the different divisions or parts as well as serving as a reminder of the overall purpose of the organization. In small organizations the articulation of a mission or objective statement may serve to focus the attention of the owner or manager and staff on what they are trying to achieve and it should not, therefore, be thought relevant only to large corporations.

Example : Mission statement for a Forte hotel————————————

- To maintain its position as the company's most profitable provincial UK hotel, (profit per room).
- To lead the Forte brand initiative by capitalizing on its prime location.
- To improve its reputation as an employer through better living and working conditions and promotional opportunities
- To respond to increased demands of clients with better standards of accommodation, food and beverage and meeting facilities. To offer improved standards of service and hospitality. (*Adapted from* Thompson, *Strategic Management* (1990), p. 109.)

5. **Objectives in non-profit making organizations**

A statement of general objectives also serves its purpose for non-profit making organizations in identifying where they are going, how they intend to get there and why they are doing so. Stakeholders, for example members of the National Trust, may need reminding of the Trust's *raison d'être*, 'promoting the permanent preservation for the benefit of the nation of lands and tenements (including buildings) of beauty or historic interest and, as regards lands, for the preservation (so far as practicable) of their natural aspect, features and animal and plant life.' To achieve this can require planning a century ahead and agreeing objectives within this constraint as well as that of the organization's resources; time-scales much longer than those of other organizations.

6. **Clarifying objectives**

It may also be useful to clarify the conflicting objectives of a number of organizations, broadly regarded as tourist attractions, such as museums which have educational and scholarly objectives in terms of their preservation of national collections and which now also have commercial objectives. The Natural History Museum in London introduced entry charges in April 1987 and in 1990 it ranked fourth in the list of the top twenty UK attractions charging admission. Similarly the Victoria & Albert Museum now charges for admission and in both these cases questions have been raised as to whether the organizations' commercial objectives will lead to the subordination of their educational aims and their role as guardians of significant national collections.

*Example : The London Zoo*_____

The well-publicized problems of the London Zoo (which in 1990 ranked ninth in the top twenty list) derive at least in part from a conflict of commercial objectives – the need to finance itself as government support was progressively withdrawn through the 1980s – with its primary purpose as set out in the charter of the Zoological Society: 'the advancement of zoology and animal physiology and the introduction of new and curious subjects of the animal kingdom' for scientific study.

7. **Objectives and resource use**

Conflicting objectives exist in all organizations, if not always on the scale discussed above and taking decisions about the objectives to be set determines how resources are allocated. In commercial organizations, profitability is invariably the primary objective: high profitability allows other objectives to be achieved. Most organizations have to operate to a minimum profit constraint and in the early stages of their development a concentration on competitive strength and efficient operations is the norm so that in the longer term greater discretion and flexibility can be enjoyed.

8. Planning

Objectives are part of the broader corporate planning of the organization. Planning is central to the success of any organization: it is the process of determining in advance what is to be accomplished and how it should be achieved. It must be framed in the light of knowledge of what is operationally possible both in terms of the organization's resources and the environment in which it operates. It defines clearly the business that the organization is involved in and the direction in which it is seeking to move. These issues are recognized as of fundamental importance for a new 'start-up' business but once a business is established the 'activity trap' of day to day pressures often means that the time and effort given to planning is sometimes dangerously neglected. In these situations the enterprise and initiative shown at start-up dissipates and crisis management results. Managers then are forced to react to problem situations rather than anticipating problems in advance and the entrepreneurial search for opportunities is abandoned. There is substantial evidence to indicate that successful organizations are good at planning and use it as a vehicle for challenging management, motivating staff and controlling activity. An understanding of the current situation in which the business finds itself is a starting point for action planning.

9. Situation analysis

There are a number of analytical tools available to managers: the one most commonly used, formally and informally is a *SWOT analysis*. This leads the organization to investigate in detail its strengths (S), weaknesses (W), opportunities (O), and threats (T) thereby revealing the best way in which it can match its strengths to the opportunities available in the environment. There is, for example, no point in deciding to expand a facility if you do not have the resources to do so, whether they be financial or human. Nor will it benefit the business to decide on an expansion for which, because of changes in the demographic structure of society or changing consumer tastes, there is not a market or the market is one in which competitors have already developed an unassailable position.

10. **Opportunities and threats** These occur in the external environment of the organization and can be broadly categorized as:

(a) political
(b) economic
(c) social/cultural
(d) technological.

An analysis of the environmental influences which affect any business must therefore take into account:

(a) political factors such as legislation affecting the industry – in the tourism industry this will include the legislation specific to the industry concerning, for example, the status and funding of the tourist boards and increasingly, environmental legislation as well as a whole body of more general legislation concerning the safety and welfare of people at work, the production and handling of food, and regulation concerning monopolies. EC regulations and directives are also relevant;
(b) economic factors such as the level of demand, the rate of interest, capital markets and the availability of funding;
(c) social factors such as changes in tastes, patterns of work and leisure and changing demographic trends;
(d) technological developments and innovation – in the tourism industry the development of information technology, for example, has had and continues to have a significant impact.

11. **The environment and change**
In the environment as a whole not only are these factors interrelated in a complex way but they are also dynamic. Analysis has to be undertaken on an on-going basis, to ensure that changes and their likely effect on the organization's business are understood. Forecasting is an inexact science and there will always be unpredictable events but the more an organization understands the environment in which it is operating, the more it is likely to be able to achieve the match between its resources and that environment.

12. Identifying the competitive position

Within the environmental context the formulation of objectives and corporate strategy must take into consideration the behaviour of suppliers, customers and competitors. It is in this area that the work of M.E. Porter (1985) is most significant and should be taken into account. Porter has argued that profitability in any industry is determined by five factors:

(1) rivalry between existing firms in the industry
(2) threats of new entrants
(3) threats of substitutes
(4) the bargaining power of suppliers
(5) the bargaining power of buyers.

A good illustration of the threat of new entrants can be seen in the reactions of UK theme parks in 1992 to the opening of Euro Disney. Alton Towers, for example has responded by increased marketing and is seeking to develop a more branded approach. This is by no means an everyday threat in the theme park sector of the tourism industry where the high capital cost forms an effective entry barrier.

13. Strategic capability and resources

Having analyzed its environment and its competitive position in the industry, the opportunities and threats, the organization needs to look at its own strengths and weaknesses, that is its strategic capability in terms of its resources. To do this it may undertake a resource audit, that is a comprehensive survey of its assets in terms of its physical, financial and human resources and the goodwill attached to its name. It also needs to look at the way it uses its resources to produce the service – the added value it creates. Value chain analysis is a technical tool sometimes used at this stage to identify corporate strengths in combining resources to achieve a superior performance.

14. Portfolio analysis

For large organizations or conglomerates portfolio analysis should be noted here as a method of assessing the balance of their activities and the resources allocated to them. Well-known and used in this context is the Boston Consulting Group's product portfolio matrix which combines market growth rate and market share in four positions:

(a) star – products with high growth rate and high market share;
(b) question mark – products with high growth rate and low market share;
(c) cash cow – products with low growth rate and high market share;
(d) dog – products with low growth rate and low market share.

Large and diversified corporations engaged in the tourism industry aim to ensure a balanced portfolio of products; for example, the Pearson Group includes among its attractions Madame Tussaud's and Warwick Castle and has recently added Alton Towers to its portfolio. Even a small attraction may find it useful to apply the concept to its services.

15. Identifying competitive advantage
When a business has satisfied itself that it understands its own situation and its capabilities in relation to its environment and its competitors it is then in a position to identify the strategic options open to it. That is, what courses of action are open to it in determining its future actions, the direction in which it decided to go and its *generic strategy*, the basis on which it chooses to develop its business to give it a competitive advantage.

16. Porter's generic strategies
The work of M.E. Porter (1985) is significant again here. He has argued that there are only three generic strategies that companies can follow to create and maintain a competitive advantage: these are *cost leadership, differentiation* and *focus*.
The choice of cost leadership means that the company uses its resources to achieve lower costs than its competitors; differentiation means that the company has a range of products and services to offer, each tailored to different segments of the market; while a focus strategy concentrates on one or a few segments, offering either cost leadership or differentiation within that segment or segments.

17. Strategic option
Competitive strategy represents one part of the organization's overall strategy. Organizations also have to choose the strategic direction in which they wish to go, where there are a number of options:

(a) doing nothing;
(b) consolidating existing position;
(c) withdrawal;
(d) product/service development;
(e) market development;
(f) market penetration;
(g) diversification – related or unrelated.

18. Evaluation of options
This depends on the assessment of each option against the criteria of suitability, feasibility and acceptability.

19. Realizing objectives
Managers need to translate the mission and the overall strategic directions into operational realities. This requires the provision of specific goals and objectives for each department or functional area. These objectives need to be broken down into practical, specific and operational targets; quantifiable and capable of being measured over pre-set time frames. Business plans which are draw up to give effect to the objectives have to differentiate between the long term and the short term: formal plans for the long term are usually drawn up for a five-year period and short-term plans on an annual or seasonal basis.

20. A hierarchy of objectives
Objectives can usefully be presented in the form of a hierarchy: at the top or apex are the mission and strategic long-term objective(s), working down through divisional objectives to individual objectives. The process of setting objectives varies from one organization to another; it can be *top-down* – that is decided at the top and transmitted down, on the basis that only senior management have the 'helicopter' view of the organization and its overall strategy; or *bottom-up* with individuals setting their own objectives and presenting them to the next level above. It is generally accepted that people feel a greater commitment to objectives they have had some part in setting so that a combination òf these approaches is most desirable. What is important is that one level of objectives fits with another in working towards the overall goals of the organization.

21. Integrating objectives
Similarly it is vital that the objectives set by and for one functional area are integrated with another, so that marketing

objectives, for example, relate to those of the operations function and managers work closely together to achieve them.

22. Setting targets

Clearly stated objectives are essential and wherever possible they should be verifiable, that is it should be possible to see that they have been achieved. Quantifiable targets are set in annual budgets: increased turnover, for example, through higher visitor numbers and at the same time by greater productivity achieving a reduction in costs can be quantified in numerical terms. Targets set should be realistic; nothing can be more demotivating than failure to achieve over-ambitious targets.

23. Management By Objectives

All managers work to a greater or lesser extent to objectives but some organizations have installed a formal system of Management By Objectives (MBO). Increasingly however they have found that at a time of rapid change in the environment the system introduces too many rigidities and inflexibilities.

24. Adapting for change

The weaknesses of MBO does not mean, however, that organizations do not need objectives. Goals which are clearly identifiable, reasonable, consistent, verifiable and capable of being appraised (*see* Chapter 12) are essential for effective management. There must also be a provision to retain flexibility within the system to ensure that it continually adapts to the changing external environment.

Progress test 3

For students

S1. Why is it essential for top management to devote time and effort to setting objectives? **(1, 20)**

S2. Why are mission statements drawn up? What information is likely to be included? **(2, 3)**

S3. Obtain a copy of a mission statement issued by a tourist organization.

Examine the content and identify the stakeholders to whom it is addressed. **(2, 3)**

S4. 'A non-profit making organization does not need objectives.' True or false? Justify your answer with examples. **(1–5)**

S5. Objectives, even in profit-orientated organizations can sometimes conflict. Explain using examples from the tourism industry why this might occur and set out how such conflicts might be reconciled. **(7)**

S6. Assess the contribution a SWOT analysis could make in reassessing the strategy for a tourist attraction. **(9, 10)**

S7. Select a tourist facility with which you are familiar and identify the environmental forces which directly influence and affect its performance. **(10)**

S8. How might portfolio analysis be used by tourist attractions? **(14)**

S9 Assume that you are the managing director of a tourist attraction located in your area. Set out what you believe would be an appropriate set of objectives. **(18, 24)**

S10. Set out the sequence of activities that would need to be undertaken to produce a corporate plan for a tourist facility. **(1–24)**

For managers and practitioners

M1. How are the overall objectives set in your organization? How much time and effort is allocated to this activity? **(1, 20)**

M2. Analyze the mission statement of your organization. To what extent do you think this is a public relations exercise? Or does it really reflect the reality of work within your organization? **(2, 3, 4)**

M3. Identify the stakeholders who are interested in the performance of your organization and assess the extent to which their interests conflict. **(1–5)**

M4. Undertake a SWOT analysis for the organization in which you work. Present your findings in the form of a report that would be useful to top management. **(9, 10)**

M5. Identify the major external environmental influences that affect the operation of your facility. **(10)**

M6. Ascertain whether portfolio analysis is undertaken in your organization. Set out the benefits and problems inherent in such an activity. **(14)**

M7. Are clear objectives specified for each unit/department in your organization? Assess the benefits and drawbacks that derive from the procedures used. **(1, 20)**

M8. Assume you are the managing director of a tourism facility. Set out an appropriate procedure that you would recommend for drawing up a corporate plan. **(1–24)**

M9. Assume you are the manager of a leisure facility in a popular tourist area. Set out the factors that are likely to be of major significance when determining the overall objectives for the centre. **(1–20)**

4
Designing organizational structures

1. The significance of organizational structures

Managerial activities are carried out within a framework provided by the organization's structure. An organizational structure is necessary in all organizations employing more than a few people principally for the following reasons:

(a) to provide a means of achieving the organization's objectives by coordinating activities and tasks;

(b) to establish the relationships between the different parts of the organization, for example marketing and finance;

(c) to define clearly the lines of communication between one part of the organization and another and between one level and another;

(d) to identify sources of authority, decision making and responsibility in the organization;

(e) to establish the pattern of control laid down in the organization;

(f) to help in clarifying individual job activities and responsibilities.

The structure of the organization plays a significant part in decision making by providing the channels of communication through which information passes and by delineating responsibility for the allocation of resources. It therefore provides the framework and an integrating mechanism for the transformation of resources into output using the systems model featured in this book.

2. The organizational chart

The formal structure of an organization is sometimes drawn out in an organization chart, showing the different hierarchical levels and the distribution of functions and/or activities. Such a chart encapsulates the way the organization has arranged its work and its people *at that time* but there are several important points to make in relation to such a chart. The first is that increasingly organizations have to change and adapt to their dynamic environments and that too rigid a structure prevents them doing so. No organization chart will or indeed should, therefore, represent an accurate portrait for very long. It is also unlikely that such a chart will present a comprehensive picture of all the features of the organization's structure. It depicts the *formal* structure of the organization and along side it there will be a network of informal links that people create among themselves; these may be as significant or even more significant than the formal structure laid down in the processes of communication, information channelling and decision making in the organization.

3. Analyzing organizational structures

Organizational structures have been and are evolutionary, changing in response to the needs of the enterprise and the people in it. In analyzing them we can usefully identify a number of dimensions which are present to a greater or lesser extent in the different organizational structures. The most significant of these are:

(a) *specialization* – the extent to which work and tasks are specialized and require people with particular skills;
(b) *standardization* – rules and policies laid down as procedures to be followed in certain circumstances;
(c) *formalization* – the extent to which such rules and procedures are written down;
(d) *centralization* – the extent to which decisions are made by and authority rests with a few senior people.

4. Centralized and informal structures

Bearing these dimensions in mind let us look at the main forms of structure which have evolved and their advantages and disadvantages. In a small organization, and we have already seen how numerous these are in the tourism industry, the functions which a structure answers (*see* 4:1) can be dealt with informally. Work and responsibilities can be allocated on an ad hoc basis and the manager or owner, the source of all authority in the organization, will take major decisions. This is a highly centralized and informal structure, characterized by some writers as entrepreneurial.

5. Centralized and formal structures

When an organization grows, however, it soon reaches the

point when a more formal allocation of tasks and responsibilities is necessary. The *functional structure*, where work is divided according to function evolved, is shown in Figure 4.1.

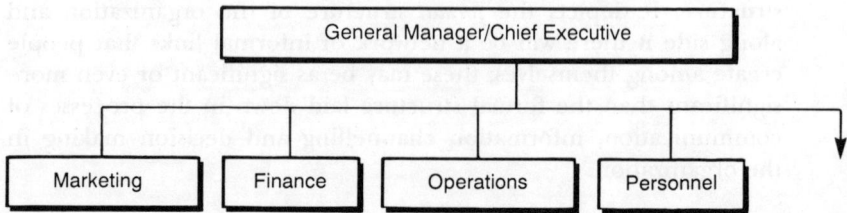

```
                    ┌─────────────────────────────────┐
                    │  General Manager/Chief Executive │
                    └─────────────────────────────────┘
        ┌──────────────┬──────────────┬──────────────┬──────────────→
   ┌─────────┐   ┌─────────┐   ┌─────────┐   ┌─────────┐
   │Marketing│   │ Finance │   │Operations│  │Personnel│
   └─────────┘   └─────────┘   └─────────┘   └─────────┘
```

Figure 4.1 *A functional structure*

This is a centralized and formal structure. Below the managers of marketing, finance, operations and personnel who report to the general manager there will be as many layers of middle and junior managers as the organization requires or its operations warrant.

It has the advantages of simplicity but the weakness of such a structure becomes apparent when the organization grows and diversifies its services.

6. Conglomerate structures

Some large companies or conglomerates which have grown through the acquisition of other businesses have adopted the relatively simple expedient of keeping the companies they have acquired as subsidiaries and within each one a functional structure. Lines of communication, control and authority between the subsidiary and the parent determine how much autonomy the subsidiary company has (*see* Figure 4.2). The Pearson Group runs its various interests in the tourism industry which include Madame Tussaud's, Warwick Castle and Alton Towers as separate companies. The parent holding company may provide some centralized services and procedures can be formalized throughout such a group to ensure a degree of uniformity and standardization. Such a structure can also provide an integrating mechanism where a subsidiary company is majority rather than wholly owned. It can however also result in considerable duplication of functional specialists within each company.

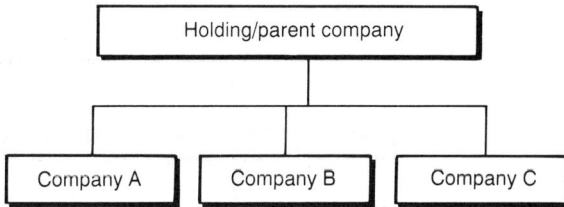

Figure 4.2 *A holding company structure*

7. Product-based and service-based structures

Organizations offering a number of services or products found as they grew and developed that it was more rational to structure their activities according to their products or services. They therefore created divisions for each product or service. An organization such as the Forte company (formerly Trusthouse Forte) splits its activities into hotels as one division (which may be sub-divided according to the class of hotel, luxury or economy, and/or by location – i.e UK and international) and restaurants as another independent division, with industrial catering as yet another division. Such divisions are decentralized and are often profit centres in their own right; that is they are responsible for their own costs and their own profitability (*see* Figure 4.3). This is regarded as desirable since their control and performance are easier to measure and relative comparisons can be made within the organization. This has important implications for motivation.

8. Spatial-based structures

Some activities in the tourism industry lend themselves to divisionalization of their activities on geographical lines. Hotels and transport enterprises, such as a national coach company, for example, may find that this proves the most efficient way to structure their activities. The National Trust operates through a network of regional offices. It is also possible to divisionalize services according to customers or to have a mix of types of service and geographical or regional bases. Weaknesses may develop through conflict between divisions for resources, or through a failure to coordinate properly. There may again be duplication of functional specialists within the division.

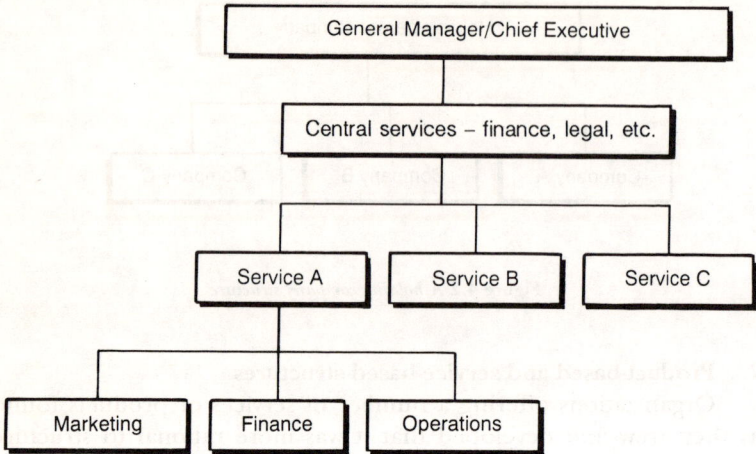

Figure 4.3 *Product and/or similar based structures*

9. The matrix structure

Matrix structures were evolved to try to combine the benefits of decentralization gained by divisionalization with greater coordination. The concept developed from team working on projects and is closely related to the ideas of team or group working (*see* Chapter 5). Such a structure may, through the establishment of dual reporting, combine product and geographical divisions or a functional and divisional structure (*see* Figure 4.4).

The major disadvantages that have emerged with matrix structures have been the blurring of lines of responsibility, lengthier decision making processes, creeping bureaucratization and sometimes an increase in the number of jobs.

10. Managing effectively

The matrix structure is a long way away from the principles laid down by the writers of the classical school who particularly emphasized that there should be a single chain of command running from the top to the bottom of an organization. They also suggested that the span of control – that is the number of subordinates any manager supervises – should be limited and that no manager should have more than five or six subordinates whose work interlocks. It is now recognized that the nature of managerial

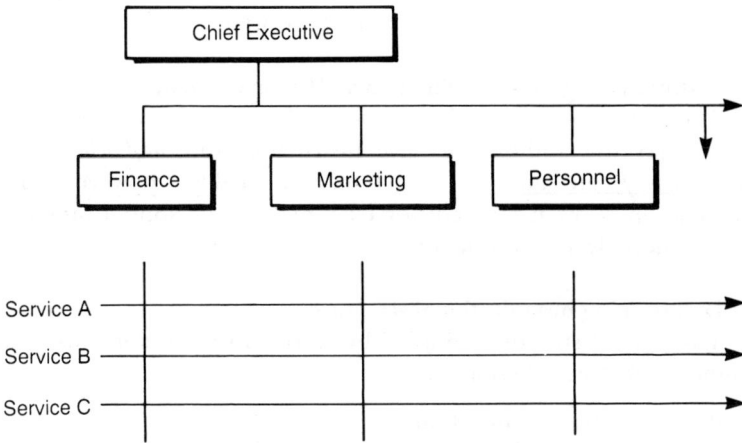

Figure 4.4 *Matric structure*

supervision depends on the scope and character of the work and that spans of control can be widened, enabling the number of levels in an organization to be reduced. Growing organizations tend to multiply hierarchical levels, a tendency that needs to be watched and checked wherever possible since long hierarchies and narrow spans of control offer people little opportunity for initiative and discretion (*see* Chapter 8). A manager can supervise a much larger number of subordinates who are doing the same job. For example, a regional manager in a hotel group can and often does supervise more than five or six hotel managers because their work does not interlock but one replicates another. The number of subordinates that can be controlled by one manager depends on their competence and skills, the complexity of their work and the manager's ability to delegate.

11. Defining spans of control

The spans of control in an organization play a part in determining the number of levels in the organization's hierarchy and in defining whether it is a tall or a flat structure. Child (1988) has suggested, on the basis of considerable empirical research, that the number of levels in an organization's hierarchy is directly related to the organization's size and that broadly speaking an organization employing about 200 people would need four levels, an organization employing about 1,000 may need six levels and for 10,000 seven or eight levels would be appropriate.

12. Distinguishing between line and staff management

There is also a distinction to be made between *line jobs*, those which carry the authority to give instruction and *staff jobs*, those which carry an advisory function. In reality, however, the demarcation is often blurred; for example, the personnel function was traditionally a staff function.

13. Determining organizational structure

The type of structure adopted by an organization depends on a number of factors. These include:

(a) the size of the organization;
(b) its strategic objectives;
(c) the nature and scope of its business;
(d) the type of technology it uses;
(e) its geographical dispersion;
(f) the market and environmental conditions in which the business is operating – how stable or unpredictable they are;
(g) the culture of the organization, that is the set of attitudes and values which have become the accepted norms in that organization;
(h) its history, development and evolutionary stage.

14. The functional model

An organization's choice of structure must seek to encompass the diversity of its objectives, its activities and the people working within it, taking into account the factors enumerated in **13** above. Figure 4.5 shows a functional-type structure for a museum which is not untypical. Because the museum is the responsibility of the local authority, finance is not a major function and the general manager will take such responsibility as is delegated to him for finance as well as dealing with personnel matters.

15. The case of Lancelot House

The following example illustrates the diversity of operations undertaken by many tourist facilities and hence the difficulty of designing a uniquely correct organizational structure. A structure needs to provide unity and harmony particularly if there are diverse interests between the stakeholders.

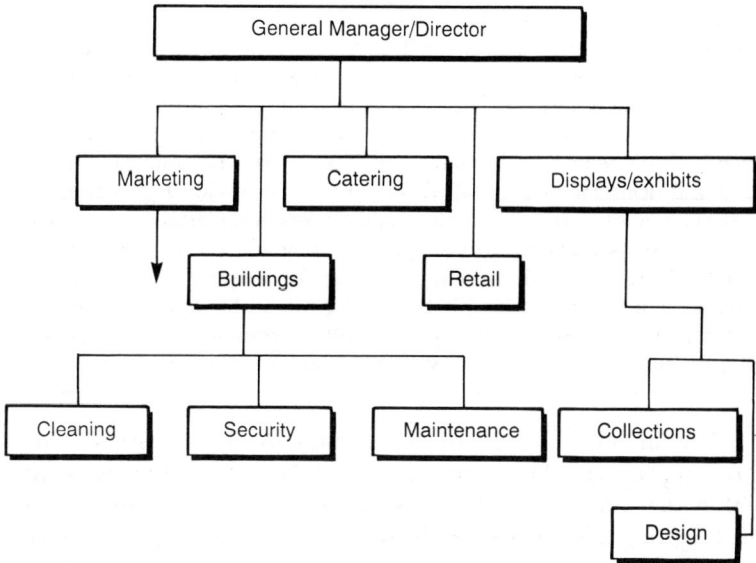

Figure 4.5 *A museum with a functional structure*

Example : Lancelot House

Lancelot House was originally a large and rich Benedictine monastery with an extensive estate. It was acquired, at the dissolution in 1539, by the Fauntleroy family who owned it until recently. They preserved much of the original building and added extensions in the eighteenth and nineteenth centuries. Members of the family have figured prominently in English history as politicians and rebels since their arrival with the Norman conquest, gradually increasing the family's wealth and position by means of strategic marriages. The house and gardens were opened to the public soon after the last war when taxation forced the then Lord Fauntleroy to seek a way of retaining the family estate. Exhibits included an account of the part family members have played in English history, as well as furniture, pictures and so on acquired in its heyday. More recently the family have added additional facilities to increase the attraction of Lancelot to tourists. The country's largest collection of aeroplanes is housed there, accompanied by an exhibition showing episodes in the history of aviation and the technical development of the aeroplane. Seeing what appeared to be an opportunity in the marketplace the Fauntleroys also built a conference centre with all the necessary facilities.

The present Lord Fauntleroy, who inherited the estate two years ago, works abroad and is not interested in it as a business enterprise. Long and complicated negotiations have resulted in an agreement with Heritage Properties who are to manage the facility on a long lease, paying an agreed percentage of profits to the owner. They will be constrained by conservation and heritage legislation as to what they can do to the property but they plan to make it a much more commercial enterprise. There will be two shops selling kitchenware and herbs, gifts and souvenirs and four food and drink facilities installed on the site. Permission has been granted to develop a water sports complex on the lakes of the estate, some distance from the house. There are also plans to upgrade the conference centre and to develop a small airfield to reflect the interest in aviation. Flying lessons, helicopters and hot air ballooning will all be available with special events featured. Two hundred people will be employed full-time, another 50 part-time and extra seasonal staff employed from time to time.

For an organization this size a functional structure would be most appropriate but there are a number of options as to how, within that framework, the work could be arranged. The priorities in designing a structure would be to keep it as simple as possible since this is not a really large organization and to keep it as flexible as possible so that adaptation and change are possible (*see* Figures 4.6 and 4.7).

This structure (Figure 4.6), it might well be argued, would give the operations manager far too wide a span of control. More senior managers for catering and retail would be an alternative, while the general manager could take responsibility for finance and personnel (*see* Figure 4.7):

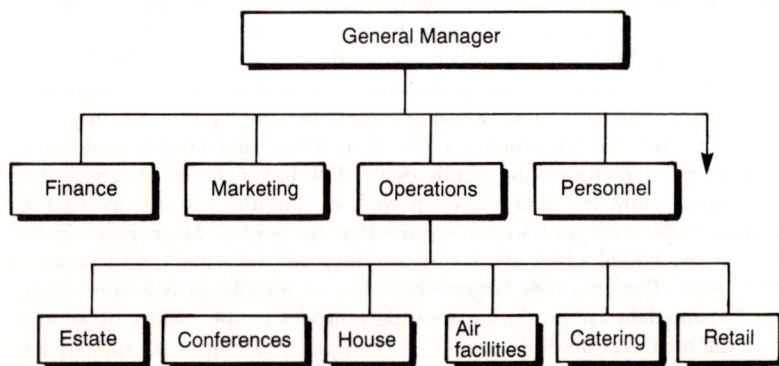

Figure 4.6 *Option 1 for Lancelot House*

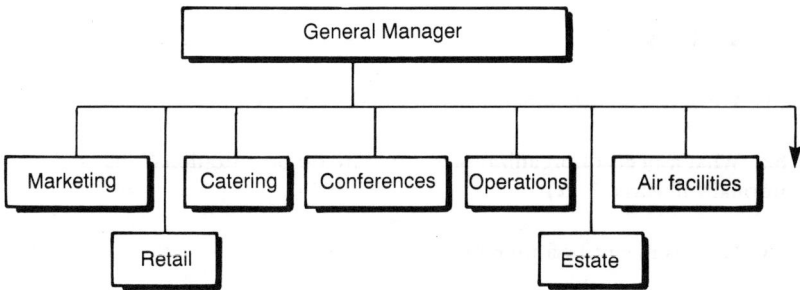

Figure 4.7 *Option 2 for Lancelot House*

In this model the marketing manager would need to work laterally with the retail, catering and conference managers. The operations manager will require specialist managers for the house and for the collections and he will retain responsibility for security, safety, maintenance and cleaning. The estate manager will require specialists in gardening and water sports to report to him.

16. Structural diversity

This example illustrates an important aspect of organizational structures: there is no one perfect structure for any organization. Whichever of the models indicated above – or some variation of them – was installed at Lancelot House in the first instance it would require constant review and possibly adaptation as the facility developed. It would only become clear during the course of its operations whether the structure was working satisfactorily or if it was causing problems. Another point to consider would be whether it permitted expansion and growth. The most appropriate structure for any organization is the one which enables the organization to achieve its objectives and secure operational efficiency. It should also provide a framework in which the individual jobs can fit comfortably. Unsuitable or outdated structures cause dissatisfaction and inefficiency. A good organizational structure does not guarantee good performance from those working in it but a poor structure, unsuitable for the organization, makes good performance impossible.

Progress test 4

For students

S1. Why are organizational structures necessary? **(1)**

S2. What aspects of organizational structure do organizational charts normally illustrate? **(2)**

S3. What is meant by a functional structure? **(5)**

S4. Why are product- or service-based structures used? **(7)**

S5. Why are divisions based on geographical lines frequently found in the tourism industry? **(8)**

S6. Enumerate the advantages and disadvantages of a matrix structure. **(9, 10)**

S7. Identify the factors that are most influential in determining organizational structures. **(13)**

S8. Collect two or three organizational charts from organizations in the industry. Give explanations for your findings. **(1–16)**

For managers and practitioners

M1. Draw an organizational chart for the organization in which you work. Explain why it has evolved in this way. **(1–3)**

M2. To what extent does the formal organizational chart represent the way the organization works? Is there an informal network also operating? **(2, 3)**

M3. Can you suggest ways your organization might be restructured? **(5, 6, 7, 8, 9)**

M4. Obtain copies of the organizational charts of other operators in your sector. Compare and contrast your findings. **(5, 6, 7, 8, 9)**

M5. Which of the influential factors identified in the text have been most influential in determining your organization's structure? **(13)**

M6. Critically assess the extent to which the organizational structure used in your organization facilitates or impedes good performance. **(16)**

5
Designing jobs

1. Defining a job

We may define a job as the task or tasks that individuals must perform to play their part in achieving the organization's objectives. The nature of the task(s), the extent of the skill(s) required of the individual and the amount of discretion he or she has in the way the job is performed are largely determined by the organization's structure. The more formalized and centralized the organization is, the less discretion the individual is likely to have because the more procedures will be laid down. The other significant dimension of the job is the extent to which it is specialized, either in the sense that it is limited to one activity or part of a task that is performed again and again; or in the sense that the job consists of a task or tasks that require specialist, sometimes technical, skills. For example, this is a feature of some areas of management information systems or accounting.

2. The role of the job description

Most organizations rely on job descriptions to define particular jobs for clarification of who is doing what in the organization. They are also essential for the purposes of recruitment and selection, training and reward systems, performance review and appraisal, staff development and career progress and planning (*see* Chapter 8). The analysis of the job which precedes the drawing up of the job description should therefore be carried out carefully, using all the information available from the person doing the job, from his/her superior and from other people in the organization who are significant contacts for the performance of that job.

3. Designing the job description

The essential information in the job description may be set out as shown in Fig 5.1.

Job title: to indicate the nature of the job.

Department:

Salary/wage range:

Duties and responsibilities: the scope of the job with as much detail as possible and when the holder has several responsibilities it is necessary to quantify as much as possible the amount of time it is anticipated that each will take.

Reports to: job-holder's immediate superior.

Responsible for : job-holder's subordinates – number and job-titles.

Limitations on authority: these may be financial such as putting a figure on the amount the job-holder can spend without seeking further authority or procedural on for example staff matters – subordinates' holidays.

Other contacts: working relationships with other functional areas which are of major significance to the job.

Date of job description: important because in a changing organization the responsibilities of a job may change and the description require adjustment and up-dating.

Figure 5.1 *Layout for a job description*

4. The job description in context

The job description may be written in whatever way seems appropriate and helpful to the particular organization. Traditionally jobs have been described in terms of duties and responsibilities but it has been suggested that rewriting duties in terms of the anticipated outcome may lead to a clearer understanding of the tasks to be carried out, why they are to be accomplished and a more obvious alignment with the objectives they are intended to achieve.

5. The job specification

An extension of the job description is the job specification. This sets out the skills, competences and attributes required to do the job. Accurate job analysis results in a clear identification of the knowledge, experience and expertise required. Formal qualifications, physical characteristics, technical skills, experience and any special demands should be distinguished. These are often ranked in importance or designated as essential or desirable. The job specification is of major use when recruiting and selecting for a job, enabling a profile of the qualities, personality and attributes of the ideal person for the job to be drawn up, but increasingly, as organizations change and adapt to rapidly changing environments, jobs also change and the job specification may identify gaps in the knowledge or skills of the present holder which can be filled by training.

6. **Using the competence concept**
   An increasing number of businesses are starting to use the competences concept to identify the skills and abilities required for the completion of tasks. The identification of the generic competences required by management has been supported by the Management Charter Initiative along with the idea of minimum attainment levels. The breaking up of a competence such as, for example, the ability to communicate orally, into different aspects, ranging from the ability to listen actively to others, to the ability to speak with ease and clarity in presenting arguments logically, enables a clearer analysis of what level is required by a particular job.
   Similarly team-building skills may range from the basic ability to comprehend the interests of team members to the more positive and creative ability to foster the skills of individual team members to achieve the resolution of problems and the achievement of team objectives.

7. **Defining the job function**
   Early management theory suggested that greater efficiency could be achieved by breaking jobs down to the simplest task and recruiting specifically for that task. Since then a body of research has shown that such a course of action does not lead to more efficiency but rather results in boredom and dissatisfaction. Alternative ways of designing jobs to provide for greater variety and greater satisfaction have been sought.

8. **Job enlargement**
   Job enlargement increases the scope of a job by adding to the number of tasks and creating greater variety within it. There is

however little evidence that job enlargement in isolation acts as an incentive for better performance although it sometimes increases job satisfaction.

9. Job rotation

If practised as a variation of job enlargement, with tasks being alternated over a period of time, job rotation produces much the same effect. It should be noted, however, that in the tourism industry, particularly in smaller facilities or attractions that only employ a small number of people, job rotation is a significant way of deploying staff and of offering variety in what are inevitably a number of routine tasks. At the Oxford Story, for example, a small core staff is permanently employed, supplemented by part-timers at peak periods with whom tasks are shared. As part of a team loyalty and commitment can be generated.

10. Job enrichment

It is widely accepted, however, that job enrichment can provide as its name suggests an enriching experience for the employee and can provide jobs which are more motivating. Job enrichment should:

(a) remove some of the controls from the job while retaining accountability;
(b) increase the individual's accountability for his/her own work;
(c) give more authority to the individual and more freedom in the sense of the scope to arrange his/her own work schedule;
(d) add new and more complex tasks to the job, giving the individual the chance to grow and develop skills.

Overall, job enrichment should give greater responsibility, opportunities for achievement and recognition and openings for growth, learning and development.

11. Delegation

Giving individuals greater responsibility and accountability involves delegation, an essential function of management but one that many managers find difficult. The extent to which a manager can delegate tasks to his subordinate(s) will be in part determined by the nature and design of the organization's structure. The extent of formalization and centralization (*see* Chapter 4) may limit the amount of delegation possible as will the degree of flexibility in the structure and, in large organizations, the amount of bureaucracy. As a general rule delegation is easier in small organizations in the private sector, of which there are many in the tourism industry. Other characteristic features of the industry (*see* Chapter 1) such as the unpredictable and unprogrammable behaviour of people which necessarily requires of the staff dealing with the customer an ability to be flexible, to cope with the unforeseen and to respond to unusual situations and demands necessitate delegation of responsibility to frontline staff.

12. Obstacles to delegation

Delegation involves belief on the part of the manager who delegates that the subordinate will be able to achieve the task(s) delegated and the confidence of the subordinate that he/she will be trusted to do the task that has been delegated. There are, however, obstacles to delegation on both sides which can easily become institutionalized and inhibit delegation, leaving managers over-worked and stressed and subordinates dissatisfied. Managers may fail to delegate not only because they lack confidence in their subordinates but also because they do not have the ability to direct the work of others. They may fear the risk of delegating work or they may simply believe that they can do it better themselves. Subordinates may not want the responsibility of additional tasks delegated because they already have enough work and they do not see any reward, extrinsic or intrinsic, in doing any more, or they may lack the confidence to do it. They may feel that they have not the resources or the information to complete the task(s) satisfactorily and that if they fail their position will be worsened. Attitudes toward delegation may also be conditioned by assumptions about people and their attitudes to work (*see* Chapter 8).

13. The function of group work

If the obstacles to delegation can be overcome, tasks which will provide job enrichment on the lines indicated above can be delegated. Job enrichment may also be achieved through the establishment of work groups or teams. In most organizations there are informal groups, which the members themselves create for social or work purposes. More formal groups are established sometimes for a specific project such as for example developing a new product or service which may involve people from different functions. Empirical research about the nature of human behaviour in the organizational framework has suggested that groups can be a useful way of coordinating activities and achieving objectives.

14. Establishing groups

To perform effectively a group needs to be cohesive. It passes through various stages of establishing relationships within the group which enable it to achieve that cohesiveness described by Tuckman (1965) as:

(a) *forming* – the initial stage when the group members get to know each other and begin to take on roles

(b) *storming* – members challenge each other and the views put forward about how to carry out the task

(c) *norming* – rules and procedures are agreed

(d) *performing* – cohesiveness is achieved and the group can work effectively.

15. Belbin's group model

Within any group members take on different roles. The work of R. M. Belbin (1981) at Henley on groups led him to suggest a model of eight different roles created a balanced team which would perform effectively. The roles are:

(a) the chairman – the social leader of the group, guides and coordinates

(b) the shaper – the task leader

(c) the plant – the imaginative ideas person – has to be nurtured

(d) the monitor – the analytical checker of the group

(e) the company worker – the organizer

(f) the resource investigator – the fixer

(g) the team worker – conflict resolver, mediator

(h) the finisher – keeps the group to schedule.

The structure and pattern of relationships in the group will be to some extent determined by the nature of the task(s) the group has to perform. The dynamics of group behaviour is an area that has attracted a good deal of research attention in recent years and is likely to continue to do so. Groups provide a way for cross functional, task-orientated working which is particularly relevant within the tourism industry.

16. The role of groups within the organization

Groups work within an organizational structure and their

activities will reflect and must integrate with the process of management and leadership within the organization. Leadership is not necessarily synonymous with management – in other words all managers are not leaders – but managers are concerned with leadership in groups, in the wider context of the organizational structure and in the design of individual jobs.

17. The nature of leadership

There have been many attempts to define the nature of leadership, focusing on the qualities of leaders and the situations in which leadership is exercised. The approach which seems to have been most useful and gained a good deal of acceptance in the management world in recent years is that of John Adair (1983). He has suggested in an action-centred leadership model that to be effective a leader must meet three interrelated areas of need – *task, team maintenance* and *individual* – represented as three overlapping circles as in Figure 5.2.

Figure 5.2 *Action centred leadership model*

18. Management style

The way in which leaders or managers behave within the organization is also determined by the style which they adopt. The extreme, at one end of the spectrum, can be characterized as authoritarian and at the other democratic. Authoritarian managers tell subordinates what to do; democratic managers join in decision making with subordinates. In between there are the managers who sell, or persuade subordinates about the decision they wish to take or consult with them about the decision.

19. Organizational culture
Managerial style also reflects the organization's culture, which is also evidenced in its rituals and routines and broadly may be described as 'the way we do things here'. The prevailing values, attitudes, norms and beliefs which make up the culture play a part in determining and influencing the behaviour of individuals within the organization.

20. The Blake and Mouton Managerial Grid
Another approach to managerial style is presented by the Blake and Mouton Managerial Grid (Blake and Mouton 1964) which allows for eighty-one different style positions measured by two dimensions: concern for people and concern for the task or production. The grid is made up of a vertical axis measuring concern for people from 1 (low) to 9 (high) and a horizontal axis showing concern for production from 1 (low) to 9 (high). The style chosen and adopted by any manager on this grid will be determined by a mixture of factors including the organizational structure, the manager's own attitudes and beliefs and the style he/she has used in the past and its effectiveness.

21. The individual in context
Managerial style is one aspect of human behaviour within the organization which has to be taken into consideration when designing jobs. A balance has to be found between the individual's needs and those of the organization as a whole. Objectives have to be reconciled with individual behaviour, motivation and aspirations in the context of resource availability. This area of human resource management will be revisited in Chapter 8.

Progress test 5

For students

S1. What factors determine the amount of discretion a job-holder has ? (1, 11)

S2. Write a job description for a job in a tourism business where you have worked or about which you have some knowledge. (3, 4)

S3. Extend this into a job specification, emphasizing and identifying the competences required. (5, 6)

S4. Compare what is involved in job enlargement and job enrichment. (8, 9, 10)

S5. What are the advantages of delegation? (11, 13)

S6. What are the obstacles to delegation? (12)

S7. List the benefits and disadvantages of working in groups. (13, 15, 16)

S8. Assess the likely impact of authoritarian and democratic styles of leadership. (17, 18)

S9. Set out and consider a range of management styles using the concepts of the Blake and Mouton Managerial Grid. (20)

For managers and practitioners

M1. How much discretionary power is there in your job ? Consider whether you would like more discretion and whether this would be possible in your organization? (1, 11)

M2. What use is made of job descriptions and job specifications in your organization ? (3, 4, 5)

M3. Do job descriptions and job specifications reveal any gaps in your knowledge/skills/competences and, if so, how could they be remedied? (6)

M4. Is job rotation used in your organization ? If so how does it work and could it be improved? (9)

M5. Do you delegate enough? Does your manager delegate to you. If not why not? (11, 12, 13)

M6. Explain how working groups or teams are formed in your organization. (14)

M7. Does Belbin's model seem useful from your experience of working in groups? (15)

M8. What style of leadership is most common in your organization? (17, 18)

M9. Using the concepts of the Blake and Mouton Grid, what style of management do you adopt? Would another style be more effective? (20)

Part three

The product and its marketing

Introduction to part three

1 Introduction.

Marketing is central to long-term success in tourism enterprises. It involves more than the functions of promotion and selling which are sometimes superficially credited as marketing: it underpins the whole process of providing customer satisfaction. It is equally relevant to profit and non-profit orientated organizations since it plans, organizes and directs the activities necessary to meet customer needs and at the same time ensuring that the overall objectives of the organization are satisfactorily met. This involves taking the product from the initial idea stage through to the final delivery of the experience for each individual visitor/user. Recognition of the need to develop sustainable tourism re-emphasizes the necessity of integrating the marketing and planning process and their management functions within each organization.

2. Marketing

Marketing is an enormous subject and it is the one area of service industry management that has attracted a great deal of attention both from practitioners and academics. Here we focus on marketing as a management function, providing a survey of the strategic concepts, essential skills and competencies needed for effective management in this area. In the course of this, the issues and problems likely to arise in tourism attractions regardless of their size, type or location will be highlighted.

Part three

The product and its marketing

6
Market research, planning and strategy

1. How to plan successful marketing strategies

The product, as we have seen in Chapter 1, is a bundle of services + goods + environs that need to be combined appropriately to fulfil customer needs and expectations. This design exercise is fraught with difficulties. Successful marketing identifies the attributes and features specific to the attraction and so differentiates the product from that of competitors, thereby achieving the magical and much sought after competitive edge. Constructing this combination requires flair, creativity and imagination but these skills are rarely sufficient in isolation and they have to be backed up by astute analytical ability to ensure that the assembled package of service elements, image and experiences meet visitor needs and expectations.

A survey conducted by the British Market Research Bureau for Leisure Consultants to identify the factors influencing consumers 'deciding to visit' decisions interestingly concluded that operators and consumers often have quite different rankings for the influencing factors.

2. Determining consumer preferences

This requires a systematic way of dealing with the following questions regarding visitors:

(a) Who are they?
(b) Where do they come from?
(c) Why do they visit?
(d) When do they visit?
(e) What form of transport do they use?

The answers to these questions will give a partial profile of current customers but though useful the needs of potential new customers will also need to be identified. The search for information will therefore need to be addressed on an internal and an external front.

Example : **The Oxford Visitor Study 1990–91** ────────────────

Commissioned by Oxford City Council, Thames and Chiltern Tourist Board and the Oxford and District Chamber of Commerce to establish an adequate and up to date information basis about the city's visitors, the study answers most of the questions featured above. It concludes that 60 per cent of Oxford's visitors are British, 17 per cent European, 13 per cent from the USA and 10 per cent from elsewhere in the world. Overseas visitors are broken down further into country of origin. Fifty per cent of visitors are under 35 years of age, 60 per cent are in white collar occupations; the survey goes on to identify means of transport, length of stay, types of accommodation used, amount spent and numbers visiting the colleges, the Ashmolean Museum, the Oxford Story and other attractions in the city. The information gathered has considerable implications for the marketing function of the attractions as well as for the city's hospitality sector and transport planners.

3. **Data collection**

Collecting data is a time consuming and costly process so the potential benefits will need to be set against the costs. A minimum amount of information is absolutely essential otherwise decisions become mere guesswork but in reality there is also a point at which data overload can be reached. A balance is therefore necessary to ensure that the data collected can be transformed into the meaningful information that is required to underpin the marketing decisions that have to be taken en route from design to delivery.

4. **Data sources**

Data sources are varied and may include:

(a) Internal organizational data. It is often surprising to external observers how little use some organizations make of data that is readily at hand, for example, figures recording past or current visitor behaviour. Frequently responses to marketing initiatives are not recorded accurately so that a rich source of potentially very useful information is lost. The implication is that in established units data collection should be an on-going activity. In large organizations care should be taken that the documentation is coordinated as there is otherwise a danger that really useful information may be kept at a divisional or unit level and not woven into a holistic view. In small units, owners or managers often assimilate a great deal of information about their customers during operations since these frequently involve personal contact with visitors. Once alerted to the opportunities that this presents they can often compile accurate visitor profiles. Even so it is usually necessary for most organizations to have to supplement their internal data with external sources

(b) *External monitoring systems* are used to review data and information that is available on market trends and competition. The source will very much depend on the objective of the search and the level at which it is being conducted. At *international* level the World Tourism Organization (WTO) publications would be a starting point for a search in secondary sources; OECD sources are valuable for their member countries statistics and the information is usually reliable; EIU surveys cover individual countries; tourism flows in and out of the UK are recorded by the Employment Department's International Passenger Survey (IPS) and further national data on the UK is available from the UK Tourism Survey (UKTS). Both IPS and UKTS are on-going surveys so that trends can be determined. Additional statistical information can be obtained from Leisure Day Visits Survey (LDVS) conducted by the Office of Population Censuses and Surveys (OPCS) for the Department of Employment, the English Tourist Board (ETB) and the British Tourist Association (BTA). Most of this information for the UK is announced or published in the *Employment Gazette*. Visitor numbers; expenditure patterns levels and trends: seasonality; visit durations; transport; accommodation and destinations are covered. Specialized publications by research centres are also a useful source for specific data; for example, the Economic Intelligence Unit (EIU) produces *MINTEL* and other travel and tourist reports; Retail Business and Keynote publications cover some sectors; stockbrokers, banks, regional tourist boards provide additional and varied data.

(c) *Primary research.* Though published information can be a rich source of background data and a base for exploration it is invariably necessary to undertake primary research if information is needed on potential customers or in-depth aspects. Research of this nature is the core of market research to which we will now turn.

5. Market Research
    Market research is a vast topic often producing specialized texts so only a general review will be presented. Market research identifies opportunities and constraints that are inherent in the market place. It embodies a set of techniques and principles for

collating, recording, analyzing and interpreting data that can then be used as a basis for rational decision making. It is important to stress and recognize that though sophisticated techniques are available for processing quantitative data the accuracy of their results is dependent on the quality of the data that is fed into the models initially so much care has to be taken with the data collection process.

(a) Questionnaires are an obvious means of obtaining information from existing, past or potential customers. Care needs to be taken in the wording and sequence of the questions, the sample selected and the techniques used for transforming and evaluating the data (*see* Figure 6.1).

(b) Observations and audits may be used in various ways to appraise features and behaviour of visitors in their own and competitors' attractions.

(c) Panel interviews may provide insights into in-depth aspects of needs and/or behaviour. To the same end, trial or mock-up sessions can be conducted.

6.   **New product market research**

New product market research is one of the most difficult but challenging tasks. Potential visitors have to be identified.

If existing units are unable to meet the level of demand because of capacity constraints then the exercise of identifying customer needs is relatively easy because replication may be the best strategy. If, however, they are the dissatisfied customers of existing units then clear identification of the expectations gap will be necessary. For the completely new concept or novel idea, the uncertainty regarding customer response will be very high and the market research, though essential, will be difficult to plan and undertake. The danger of alerting competitors to your plans may be such that testing the market in practice may be the only option open although it is of course a high risk strategy.

7.   **Identifying market research needs**

The key to success in market research is to identify clearly the outcome required and then design a research and data collection programme that will fulfil these needs.

8.   **Planning an accurate forecasting model**

If an accurate forecasting model was required then a

**Bourton on the Water
Visitor Survey**

Date of interview: .... Interviewer: .... (Initials)

Time: .... Sampling point: ....

Type of weather today: ....

Please ask if interviewee is 12 years and older. Only continue if this is the case.

	CODE	ROUTE
Is the interviewee: Male	1	
Female	2	Q1

Q.1 Why have you come to Bourton on the Water today?	CODE	ROUTE
For business purposes	1	
To visit friends or relatives	2	
A day out	3	
Educational purposes	4	
As part of a holiday	5	
Other		Q2

Q.2 Have you visited Bourton on the Water before?		
Yes	1	Q3
No	2	Q4

Q.3 How many times have you been to Bourton on the Water before?		
....	☐	Q4

Q.4 On your trip to Bourton on the Water today are you:		
a. Visiting for the day, having travelled from home?	1	Q7
b. Visiting for more than one day and staying overnight in Bourton on the Water?	2	Q6
c. Visiting for the day but staying overnight away from home but not in Bourton on the Water?	3	Q5

Q.5 If you are staying overnight elsewhere, where did you stay last night?		
Town .... County		Q6

Q.6 a. What kind of accommodation did you use last night?	CODE	ROUTE
Hotel/motel	1	
Bed & Breakfast/Guest House	2	
Caravan/Camping	3	
Camping	4	
Self-catering Flat/House	5	
Stayed with friends or relatives	6	
Other?	☐	
b. How much did it cost approximately for you to stay in this type of accommodation last night?		
£..............	☐	
c. Where will you be staying tonight?		
– Town .... County	1	
– Same place	2	
– Don't know		
d. How long is your overall trip/holiday?		
.... days	☐	Q7

Q.7 How long have you spent in Bourton on the Water today?		
Less than 1 hour	1	
1–3 hours	2	
3–5 hours	3	
5–7 hours	4	
More than 7 hours	5	Q8

Q.8 Which attractions have you visited in Bourton on the Water today?		
Model Village	1	
Model Railway Exhibition	2	
Cotswold Perfumery	3	
Village Life Exhibition	4	
Cotswold Motor Museum	5	
St Lawrence Parish Church	6	
Bird Land	7	
Other	☐	Q9

Q.9 Have you purchased or used a guide?		
Yes	1	
No	2	Q10

Figure 6.1 *Example of a market research questionnaire*

		CODE	ROUTE
Q.10	Do you think that the facilities in Bourton on the Water are adequate? (eg. car parks, toilets, banks, shops, eating places.)		
	Yes	1	
	No	2	
	If no, why not?	☐	Q11
	....		
Q.11	What do you particularly like about Bourton?		
	1.		
	2.	☐☐☐	Q12
	3.		
Q.12	Are there any particular things you dislike about Bourton?		
	1.		
	2.	☐☐☐	Q13
	3.		
Q.13	If you could rate on a scale of 1 to 5 (with 5 being the top and best mark), how would you rate the following attributes for Bourton?		
	Pleasant	1 2 3 4 5	
	Overcrowded	1 2 3 4 5	
	Car Parking facilities	1 2 3 4 5	
	Toilets	1 2 3 4 5	
	Shops	1 2 3 4 5	
	Sign Posting	1 2 3 4 5	☐☐☐☐☐☐☐☐☐
	Cleanliness	1 2 3 4 5	
	Service/Customer care	1 2 3 4 5	
	i.e. in shops, etc.		
	Attractions to visit	1 2 3 4 5	
	Pubs	1 2 3 4 5	Q14
	Restaurants	1 2 3 4 5	
Q.14	How did you originally hear about Bourton?		
	Holiday brochure/travel shop	1	
	Word of mouth	2	
	Tourist information centre	3	
	Local radio	4	☐
	Newspaper/magazine	5	Q15
	Other		

		CODE	ROUTE
Q.15	Will you be visiting any other locations outside Bourton today?		
	Yes	1	
	No	2	
	If yes, which locations?	☐	Q16
	....		
Q.16a.	Are you alone today?		
	Yes	1	
	No	2	☐	Q17
	If no,		
	b. How many adults, including yourself, are with you in your party today? (people 16 years and over)		
	c. How many children are there in your party today? (under the age of 16 years)		
	....		
Q.17	What form of transport did you use to get to Bourton on the Water		
	Form of transport	☐	Q18
Q.18	Do you mind answering a few questions about how much you yourself have spent today in Bourton on Water?		
	Yes	1	Q20
	No	2	☐	Q19
Q.19	a. Can you tell me approximately how much it has cost you to travel to Bourton on the Water (either from home or from previous destination)?		
	£	☐	
	(Q.10 continued overleaf)		

Figure 6.1 *cont.*

		CODE	ROUTE
Q.19 b.	How much money have you yourself spent on goods and services in Bourton on the Water today? £	☐	
c.	Can you please give me an indication of the type of goods and services which you have purchased?	☐	
Q.20	What is your nationality? Country	☐	Q21
Q.21	In which town/country do you have permanent residency? Place .... County .... Country	☐	Q22
Q.22	Do you mind telling me what your occupation is? .... (If they are a student, unemployed, retired, or a housewife, probe to find out their father's occupation, intended occupation, previous occupation, or their husband's occupation respectively.)	☐ ☐	 Q23
Q.23	Would you please indicate from this card which category you fall into? Age category	☐	Q24
Q.24	Do you think you will return to Bourton on the Water again? Yes No Don't know	1 2 3	

THANK YOU VERY MUCH FOR YOUR CO-OPERATION

Figure 6.1 *cont.*

comprehensive market information system would be needed and should contain:

(a) Number of visitors, including information regarding socio-economic and demographic groupings, geographical origins and so on;
(b) Patterns of arrival through time on hourly, daily, weekly, seasonal and annual basis;
(c) duration of stay/visit;
(d) expenditure patterns;
(e) transport modes.

Points (a) to (e) are quantitative and easy to process but in addition qualitative information should also be sought on:

(f) motivation and behaviour;
(g) visitors' expectations;
(h) their responsiveness to elements of the marketing mix (*see* Chapter 7).

With this information at hand, forecasting and trend projection could be undertaken using a variety of techniques that might range from simple trend projection to more sophisticated econometric-type analytical models or qualitative models such as Delphi approaches. The actual techniques selected will depend on the purpose for which the forecast is being undertaken, the degree of accuracy required and the costs associated with uncertainty. Capacity planning and operational system design require long-term forecasts, which are the most difficult to undertake; budget and target setting need medium-term forecasts; while scheduling and day to day operations management require short-term forecasts.

9. **Focusing the market research exercise**
Specific decision making would require a more focused market research exercise. For example, if the pricing policy of an established attraction was under review then the significance of price to visitors would need to be appraised and assessed. This would require reliable quantitative data on the interrelationships of price with other variables influencing demand such as income and prices of competitors. If this could be obtained then correlation or regression analysis could be used to determine optimal price levels. If advertising for the coming season was under review then background information would have to be obtained on its impact on visitors' buying decisions, the significance of alternative media, and visitor travel patterns in order to identify the geographic area on which to focus.

Example _____

A rural attraction in the Cotswolds spent £3000 advertising on local radio in the Home Counties with no response success at all. After market research they found that visitors rarely travelled that distance and that nearer urban areas targeted the following year by press were much more responsive – and at a much reduced outlay.

A minimum level of appropriately targeted market research is therefore a prerequisite to success and underpins the success of the marketing process overall to which we now turn.

10. Marketing plans and strategy
Marketing plans and strategy will need to be formulated within the context of the mission, goals and objectives of the organization as a whole (*see* Chapter 3). As we have seen in Chapter 1, the tourism industry is operating in an external environment which is dynamic, uncertain and complex. Organizations which fail to respond to and anticipate trends in the industry find that they are forced into a passive acceptance of sub-optimal results. A pro-active marketing policy is, therefore, one of the keys to success.

11. Using SWOT analysis
Various models and techniques are available to aid the process of planning and strategy formulation. Typically a SWOT analysis might be used to ascertain the strengths (S), weaknesses (W), opportunities (O) and threats (T) that are relevant for the organization and its market setting. From this SWOT analysis, which should result in a realistic assessment of internal capability against the market appraisal, a strategy for

(a) *market segmentation,*
(b) *market targeting* and
(c) *market positioning*

should emerge. This can also be viewed as portfolio planning since it will reflect the product life cycle of existing products, competitors' performance and activity together with the socio-economic background of existing and potential customers.

12. Market segmentation, targeting and positioning
These are strategies for pro-active marketing. Segmentation involves classifying visitors into sub-groups according to features or characteristics. These may be based on demographic or socio-economic criteria: age, income, education, occupation, family structures; or the differentiation may be psychographic: behaviour patterns, lifestyle, status, degree of hedonism and so on. The nature of the product and the rationale underlying the exercise will influence the nature of the distinctive groupings: frequently they require judgement and experience although some are more transparent. The strategic issue is then to determine which

segments are to be targeted and whether the focusing is to be narrow or more widely positioned. Focusing products involves high risk but can bring huge rewards if correctly positioned relative to market needs. Undifferentiated products with a more general appeal are less risky but rarely end up as market leaders.

13. Porter's marketing options
In this context it is interesting to review the work of M. E. Porter who has argued that there are only three options open to any organization:

(a) to exercise cost leadership through size and standardization to allow price competition;
(b) to differentiate in effective, distinctive ways and so enable consumers perceptions to be manipulated; or
(c) to focus and establish market power.

Epitomized in these options are the dilemmas that occur in many service organizations where marketing managers wish to increase the value-added and the individuality of their service but where operations managers wish to minimize costs through standardization and conformity. Resolving these issues regarding segmentation, targeting and positioning is central to the formulation of the marketing mix to which we now turn.

Progress test 6

For students

S1. Why is it necessary to determine consumer preferences? **(1, 2)**

S2. Assume that you have been asked by a local tourist attraction to set up an external market information database for them. What would you include and how would you obtain the information? **(3)**

S3. Why is market research necessary? What type of routine market research activity would you recommend to be undertaken by (a) a museum; (b) a visitor centre; (c) a National Trust property? **(5)**

S4. Design a questionnaire for a heritage centre that wishes to profile its visitors. **(9)**

S5. What is a SWOT analysis? Why are they used? **(11)**

S6. What is meant by market segmentation? Give examples to illustrate your explanation. **(12)**

S7. Collect a selection of promotional leaflets produced by local attractions. Rank them on the basis of aesthetic appeal and communications effectiveness. Are they general or focused? Are they representative? **(12)**

S8. Draw up an advertisement to be placed in your local paper for (a) a farm open day and (b) a music festival. Consider the common features that you would include and the likely differences. **(1–12)**

For managers and practitioners

M1. Do you have adequate data in your organization to profile your visitors? (a) How is it collected? By whom? How often? (b) What are the main constraints and problems? **(1-4)**

M2. Examine a recent market-research activity that has been undertaken by your organization ascertaining: (a) its purpose; (b) the approach used; (c) the significance of its findings. **(5–9)**

M3. Design a visitor questionnaire that would provide the necessary information base that would be needed prior to a planned major advertising campaign. **(9)**

M4. Undertake a SWOT analysis of your organization as a basis for marketing planning. **(11)**

M5. Find out whether your organization has long-term strategic marketing plans. If not, why not? If yes, examine the process that was used. Would you have done it the same way? **(10)**

M6. Does your facility deliberately position itself through market segmentation and targeting ? What are the implications? **(10)**

M7. Analyze why tensions may arise between the operations and marketing managers in your organization. **(13)**

M8. Review the promotional literature and/or advertisements produced by your attraction or facility and compare them critically with those of your competitors. What conclusions do you come to? **(1–13)**

7

The marketing mix

1. The elements of marketing

The marketing mix involves the selection and combination of the elements of marketing in order to achieve the overall marketing objectives and goals. Traditionally in manufacturing industry the marketing mix was summarized as the four Ps: *product, price, place* and *promotion.* A seven 'P' mix was developed by B. H. Booms and M. J. Bitner in 1981 for service industries. An amended list is tabulated below:

(a) *Product* – range, quality, level, brand name, service level
(b) *Price* – level, discrimination, quality/price/perceived value
(c) *Place* – location, accessibility, environs
(d) *Promotion* – advertising, sales promotion, publicity, public relations
(e) *People/participants* – training, discretion, commitment, incentives, appearance, behaviour/attitude
(f) *Physical features* – environment, design, furnishings, colour, layout, noise
(g) *Process* – procedures, flow of activities, customer involvement

The list has been edited to include those factors most relevant to tourism activity though it is clear that the last three expand on the nature of the product. There is some debate regarding the validity of this separation into discrete compartments but it is useful as an aid to clarity. The reader is, however, warned that it should not be assumed that any of the mix of components is a distinct and separate activity. In reality they overlap, and decisions will be iterative in practice even if they are treated in a logical sequence for analysis. A visual guide to this procedure is presented in Figure 7. 1.

2. The product

Tourism products are diverse: in addition their nature is obscured by the fact that they are invariably consumed in

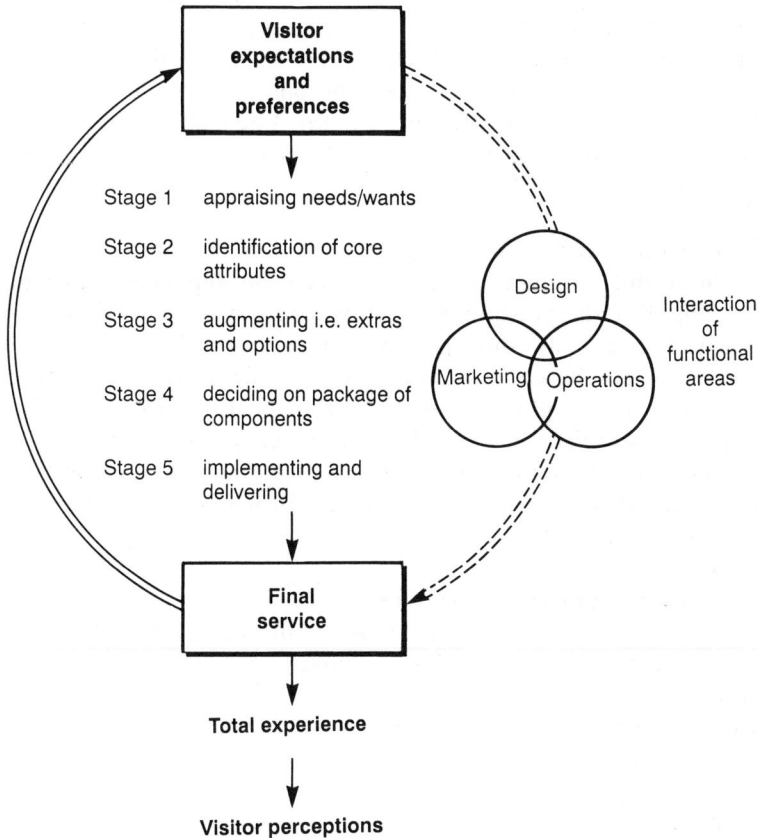

Figure 7.1 *Designing the service*

conjunction with other enabling facilities. They may also range from being natural or man-made. The focal aspect is the nature of the experience provided for the visitor. This may range from the tranquillity of a formal English rose garden in the grounds of an historic house to the educational entertainment provided by the high-tech, computer-aided models in a museum, or the thrill of a white knuckle ride in a theme park. However varied the experience, the common feature for success is that the product satisfies the customer's needs by providing the *core attributes* effectively; wherever possible augmenting these with further added value. Most attractions provide additional facilities – shops, restaurants, etc. –

which will appeal to the visitor and generate additional revenue/profits for the provider. With appropriate design and delivery these functional additions can enhance the core pull attribute and in some cases have become the main attraction. Examples of this are the restaurant at the Tate Gallery, the shop at the Victoria and Albert Museum and the conference centre at the Merseyside Maritime Museum.

3.   The importance of branding
Successful product presentation can be replicated through branding. Branding distinguishes a service from its competitors and by emphasizing its differentiation it acts as buying cue to prospective purchasers who find safety in its familiarity. Many hotel companies have exploited this strategy and it is increasingly being adopted in tourism. Center Parcs provides a classic example of branding for a holiday village in terms of the nature of its product and the associated environmental image. Disney is in the same vein at a global level.

4.   Considering market perception
Designing tourism products requires the integration of design, operations and market appeal in an imaginative way. Its perception will be assessed by users in terms of its overall value for money and in this context the next feature of the marketing mix – price – has to be examined.

5.   Price
Price is the one element of the marketing mix that generates revenue directly: all the others incur costs. The role of price as an influential variable in consumers' buying decisions can be active, passive or neutral. Deciding on the role it should play for a particular tourism attraction is a complex but fascinating process. The accuracy of the information base regarding customer preferences is absolutely crucial if it is envisaged that it is to play an active role. There are two limits to pricing:

(a) a floor which in the short run is variable cost, and
(b) a ceiling which is the amount the visitor is willing to pay.

Identifying the floor is relatively easy (*see* Chapter 9) but finding the ceiling is notoriously difficult, particularly if repeat custom is desired. From a profit-making or self-financing, organizational viewpoint charging variable cost on a long-run basis is not a viable option since all costs have to be covered. So, the question that has to be addressed is: how much can we charge over and above variable costs on some occasions, or, what can our mark-up be?

This 'cost' based approach is the norm in industry as a whole: a recent survey (unpublished) of tourism attractions revealed that the majority start from a cost base and then, looking at their competitors, determine the 'plus' that can be added. There was little evidence that the psychological aspects of pricing had been explored or experimented with although some operators recognized that 'all-in' pricing was favoured by many visitors.

There are really only three options concerning the price level:

(a) equal to the market
(b) above the market, or
(c) below the market.

The first is the easiest in time and effort since it abdicates the decision to competitors or a market leader. If on the basis of quality, image, features or reputation an attraction has no unique attributes then this in the long run may be an appropriate approach though it will not bring fame or fortune. Pricing at market level presupposes that comparative attractions exist; but they may not, and then making a price decision cannot be avoided.

Pricing above the market involves considerably more risk but can bring high rewards in terms of profits and status. It may also encourage emulators, so some uniqueness or differentiation in reality or name is absolutely essential. Care has to be taken that price thresholds are not exceeded and that customer expectations are at least adequately met.

Pricing below the market may be necessary on some occasions to compensate for such disadvantageous factors as poor location or to increase market share if visitors are price conscious. However, in the same way that high prices may go outside the customers' top price threshold, customers may become suspicious if prices are below the market norm.

Within the overall pricing strategy decisions will need to be made regarding the use of an 'all-in' price or separate prices for each facility. These may involve price discrimination on the basis of age, family grouping, party size and so on, or on time of entry according to demand patterns or regularity of use (season tickets). All these decisions will reflect the role price is seen to play in the marketing mix. Some tourist attractions of course make no charge.

Free access to cathedrals, heritage sites and nature reserves may reflect either a deliberate decision not to charge on principle or a view that at the site there is no cost-effective way to collect admission charges.

6. Place

Location is covered in detail in Chapter 10. Accessibility is one of the major determinants of success in tourism. Only if an attraction has a unique attribute or other really unusual features will visitors be motivated to overcome the locational drawbacks. The average attraction must be well situated in terms of transport facilities, customer flows and its environs if it is to attract viable numbers. Though skilful marketing may be used to offset locational disadvantages it can rarely overcome the handicap completely and the exercise is always expensive in time, energy and cost. Desirable accessible sites however will carry a premium in terms of rent or purchase price and so a balance has to be struck between the locational merits and the inherent costs.

7. Promotion

The function of promotion is to inform, persuade and influence potential customers' decisions by making them aware of the products on offer and stimulating interest into buying action. The various forms are usually used in combination although we will look at them separately.

The amount spent on *advertising* and its prominence in promotion will depend on marketing needs, customers' demands for information or their vulnerability to persuasion. The nature of the advertising used will reflect the stage in the life cycle of the product and its market setting. Informative advertising is often used in initial stages and is then followed by more persuasive pressures if competition is really fierce. Campaigns will need to be planned: they invariably take longer to set up than is originally envisaged by the inexperienced. Media selection will involve assessing the merits and limitations of press, radio, TV and other media. Clarity, style and presentation is as important as frequency, positioning and exposure. The value and relative merits of *direct mail, personal selling* and other distribution channels including exhibitions and trade shows will also need to be appraised.

Advertising and promotion are specialist areas requiring appropriate knowledge and skills. Large organizations can afford to set up special departments but small organizations should consider using reputable agencies or advisors. On average most operators spend less than 10 per cent of operating costs on advertising: although some market leaders are reputed to spend up to 15 per cent. For competitive markets such as theme parks and wildlife attractions this translates into as much as £1 per visitor. A large proportion of this involves TV promotions.

Public relations is increasingly seen as central to effective promotion for tourist organizations and it is no surprise to find that the most successful organizations devote considerable time and effort to their public image through subtle use of press releases, logo design and literature presentation. The intangibility of the product heightens the need for quality assurance and so endorsements by travel writers, feature editors or TV travel programmes become highly desirable. A small rural museum in Oxfordshire had its visitor numbers increase by well over 100 per cent in the months following a two minute feature on a travel programme. The fact that tourism products are often consumed in conjunction with other enabling facilities such as accommodation and travel means that the role of joint promotions is more relevant and can frequently be successfully developed within this sector of the industry. One aspect of promotion must however be carefully monitored: particular care must be taken that quality expectations are not hyped and raised above the levels that can be delivered in practice. The range, quality and extent of facilities must match visitors' expectations, especially if repeat custom is part of marketing strategy.

8. People

There is increasing evidence to suggest that the 'quality' rating of any attraction is closely linked to the quality of service provided by staff. Being individuals they do not conform to the standard specification laid down for machines on a manufacturing production line and in this sense quality control is a challenge. Attitude becomes all important and has to be nurtured. Commitment, courtesy and care are the hallmarks of good recruitment, training and people management (*see* Chapter 8 for detailed review of role of staff). Much of staff activity within tourist attractions is routine. The key to success is to convert what is routine to staff into a unique experience for the visitor – a challenge that is now being taken up by the most successful operators in the industry. The positive effect on staff morale is mirrored in the improvement of the bottom line. The ethos and atmosphere of the attraction is set by the people working in it and their interface with visitors: 'The moment of truth' as it is referred to by R. Normann (1991), is often the point of staff contact or encounter.

9. Physical features

Physical features are a dominating influence in all attractions and will vary according to whether they are natural or built. If natural, the features will be central to their appeal. But man-made attractions may originally have been built for use far removed from tourism (for example, castles and historic houses) and will since have been adapted in various ways. The architecture and artifacts of Blenheim are presented in a historic setting deliberately preserved so that visitors are able to appreciate the original features. In others, such as Warwick Castle, designers have used and enhanced physical features with clever design and interpretation so that the final product has a different ethos and appeal.

Purpose-built tourism attractions need to weld ergonomic and functional features with the desired ambience and image. It is a highly skilled activity and depends on good design that meets the established criteria of 'fitness for purpose'. Apart from the selection of the designers themselves they also have to be appropriately briefed with the correct specification in order to come up with the right concept. External and interior features have to be considered in the light of planning, building and safety regulations as well as the aesthetics of style, decor and colour.

10. Process

Process is the point at which customer needs are actually met and so involves the integration of all aspects of the marketing mix. Process design and delivery, therefore, needs to be a team effort involving staff from other functional areas including operations and personnel. The starting point would be to focus on the *core issue* of meeting visitor needs, which will reflect their main motivation for visiting, attending or buying and from this to identify both the *elements* and *standards* of service required. Options include:

(a) level
(b) quality
(c) degree of standardization
(d) customer involvement
(e) speed, timing, duration

(f) reliability
(g) aesthetics
(h) safety
(i) security.

Though listed separately, they will in reality overlap. Some of the options may be combined or indeed varied as a response to particular situations.

11. Striking the balance

It is at this stage that conflict may arise between the innovatory ideas of the marketeer who seeks differentiation and the more hard-nosed perspective of the operations manager who looks for standardization as a means to cost-effectiveness. A balance will need to be struck, but if the strategic issues of segmentation, targeting and positioning have been thoroughly researched then the conflicts will be easily resolved.

In some attractions the visitor is subtly controlled regarding his/her movement and progression because of space or time constraints. At Heritage Projects centres visitors are conveyed through exhibits on time controlled vehicles disguised as time carts (at Jorvik) or scholars' desks (Oxford Story). This permits the management to control the volume of throughput by adjusting journey times. Such mechanisms also impose a ceiling constraint.

Many historic houses do the same thing even though visitors appear to be free to wander. At peak times guides operate within rigid and pre-set time constraints, controlling the flow of visitors by length of presentations, door control and other devices, while during quieter periods they have greater discretion and can provide a much more personalized guiding experience.

12. Customer involvement

The introduction of customer involvement has been recognized as a means of differentiation. The 'hands-on' experiences provided in museums such as the Science or Natural History museums in London are evidence of how participation, through ingenious interpretation, can enhance enjoyment and fundamentally alter the nature of the experience. Wigan Pier is a classic example of how the sense of time and place can be reinforced by the interface between 'actors' and the public to create a unique experience enjoyed by young and old alike.

13. Coping with customer demand

Designing the process also involves decisions about capacity carrying levels. If these prove to have been forecasted inadequately and demand rises above the optimal levels then service encounter difficulties will arise and the confrontations have to be dealt with by staff at the delivery point, although in reality they are the responsibility of top management.

There are strategies that can be adopted to offset these problems, particularly if they are predictable (for instance Bank Holidays). Special events, demonstrations or other entertainments can be arranged to absorb visitors and pull them away from pressure points so that even if physical capacity is at its limit, perceptual capacity may be stretched so that reduced psychological damage is done.

14. Minding your Ps and Cs

The significance for marketing managers of these operational issues cannot be overstated and they reinforce the need for cooperation and integration of these functions at all stages.

The paradigm of 'four' or 'seven' Ps is now being questioned. Kotler (1990), a marketing guru, has suggested that marketing is about 'delighting the customer' and that an emphasis on 'Cs' might be more appropriate: *customer value* instead of product; *cost to customer* in terms of money, energy and time, instead of price; *convenience* rather than place and *communication* rather than promotion. All this adds up to providing a quality service with a customer focus. This is a topic we will return to in more detail in Chapter 11.

Progress test 7

For students

S1. Define what is meant by the 'marketing mix' and ascertain the extent to which the concept is relevant to tourism products. **(1)**

S2. Distinguish between 'core' and 'peripheral' aspects of tourism products. Illustrate your argument by using examples with which you are familiar. **(2)**

S3. Set out the main factors that should be taken into account when deciding on the prices charged in tourism enterprises. **(5)**

S4. Why is 'place', i.e. location, such an important component of the marketing mix for tourist attractions? **(6)**

S5. Collect examples of promotional activity undertaken by tourist attractions/organizations in your area. Compare and contrast the approaches used and attempt to explain the differences and similarities. **(7)**

S6. Visit a local tourist attraction and pay particular attention to the way you were treated by staff. Did they enhance or detract from the experience? Explain the reasoning behind your conclusions. **(8)**

S7. Set out why 'design' is important to tourist attractions. **(9)**

S8. Recall a recent visit to a tourist attraction. Identify the 'core' provision and the other 'elements' that were provided. Assess how they were interrelated to influence the 'experience' that was delivered. **(10)**

For managers and practitioners

M1. How many of the marketing mix Ps apply to your tourism product? **(1)**

M2. What is the 'core' component of your tourism product? To what extent is it enhanced by other features and elements? **(2)**

M3. How are pricing decisions made in your organization? On the basis of your response – do they enable the overall objectives of the organization to be met? Should they be reappraised? **(5)**

M4. Assess the merits and drawbacks of the location of your attraction. How do they influence other aspects of the marketing mix? **(6)**

M5. What type of promotional activities are undertaken by your organization? Do you evaluate the results of such activities to ascertain their effectiveness? **(7)**

M6. Visit an attraction that is viewed as one of your major competitors and monitor the quality of service provided by their staff. Compare their performance with the service given by your staff, ranking high and low score features. Now determine the action that needs to be taken. **(8)**

M7. How much emphasis is given to 'design' in your facility? Does it permeate all aspects of your public image? Identify potential areas for improvement. **(9)**

M8. Do you have prescribed 'standards of service' for the activities undertaken in your unit/organization? If so appraise them. If not, evaluate their potential. **(10)**

M9. Set out the design specification for a Tourism Information Centre (TIC) that is to be situated inside a civic building adjacent to the city centre of an historic city. Pay particular attention to the access, layout, visual aspects and overall ethos. How might your brief for the interior design differ if you were setting up a visitor information centre at the edge of a national park but in an isolated location. **(2–14)**

Part four

Resource management

Introduction to part four

We now need to look more specifically at the management functions directly related to the use of resources in the attraction or facility: people, financial and physical. The way in which these resources are combined and the extent to which they are used efficiently and effectively during the transformation process in our systems model will determine the quality and value of the final output offered to the customer.

Resource management

Introduction to part four

8
Human resource management

1. What is human resource management?
Human resource management in the widest sense involves the attraction, retention, control, motivation, reward and development of people working in the organization. The importance of human resource management in the service industries in general and in the tourism industry in particular, has already been noted. It cannot be stressed too often that staff play a vital role in all sectors of the industry. To recap on the reason their role is so essential the reader should refer back to Chapter 1 and note again that 'staff involved in providing the process are part of the product – their attitudes, behaviour and appearance contribute to consumers' perceptions' (1:12).

Their interaction with the customer determines to a large extent the perceived quality of the service the customer receives and the reputation, whether good or bad, that the attraction or facility enjoys.

2. Staff issues in a labour-intensive industry
The tourism industry, like other service industries, is labour-intensive in most sectors. Managers face the problem of ensuring a superb performance from staff who are often recruited for a season, traditionally are not well-paid and subject to a high rate of turnover. High staff turnover represents a cost to the organization, whatever its size, in terms of the management time which has to be spent on recruitment and selection, the loss of interest in training and the possible reduction in the level of service that can be offered to customers.

3. The challenge of staff motivation
Managing human resources is, therefore, an essential skill and persuading staff to improve performance an intrinsic part of the management job. To secure the best possible staff and ensure that the business obtains the best performance from them requires an understanding of the complexities of human behaviour and the

deployment of skills at all stages of the employment process from recruitment and selection through training and motivation.

4. Manpower planning

This is linked to the organization's overall strategy, plans and objectives and related to its organizational structure. It involves an analysis of existing staff resources, forecasts of future needs and, in the case of large organizations, can also involve the use of sophisticated techniques to establish career plans and paths for individuals over a period of years. In small organizations manpower planning is of necessity a simpler operation, often carried out in the owner's or manager's head. It is, however, no less important for the manager of a small facility to be aware of the implications in human resources terms of his future plans, particularly if they involve expansion or offering new services, providing incentives for able staff to stay with the business. Until relatively recently few organizations in the tourism industry had established clear career paths, a factor still difficult in small and medium-sized organizations.

5. Recruitment and selection

Procedures for staff selection require time and careful attention. Recruitment campaigns need to target the areas of the population identified as possible sources of staff, for example mature women, perhaps with an expertise in languages. The need for this has been enhanced by current demographic trends which have resulted in fewer young people being available for employment in the early 1990s.

6. Investment in the future

Good recruitment and selection policies and procedures can go some way to reducing the problem of high turnover. Management time spent on recruiting and selecting should therefore be regarded as an investment and like all investment be accompanied by careful preparation.

7. Techniques for personnel selection

Job descriptions, job analysis, job and people specifications (*see* Chapter 5) all help to ascertain clearly the skills and competences required as well as the personal characteristics needed for a particular job. There are a number of techniques available for selection purposes including personality testing and group exercises. Each organization will have its own favourites. It is important too that candidates should have the opportunity to learn as much as possible about the job and the organization, the downside as well as the good points.

8. **Induction**
An induction period can play an important role in ensuring that new recruits become part of the organization quickly and understand its systems. Factual aspects regarding operations, safety procedures and other organizational expectations are best dealt with at induction. Clarity in conveying to new recruits their responsibilities, tasks and authority will help to prevent confusion and reduce the time it takes them to get into the job. A comprehensive staff manual is invaluable as an ongoing reference. It is at this time that the culture of an organization can be effectively imbued in staff so standards must be very clearly defined and role models set. It is particularly important that all staff – permanent, seasonal, full and part-time are included in induction programmes.

9. **The manager as motivator**
It is part of the managers' job to motivate their staff. It is generally accepted that the more the manager understands what motivates people to work and the nature of the satisfaction they obtain from their work, the better he or she will be able to provide a framework which will contribute to the quality of the organization's service. The precise relationship between motivation and job satisfaction remains unclear. It is not always the case that the more satisfied or happy that people are in their jobs, the better the performance they turn in. This is an extremely complex area and despite a mass of research and theories there is no single prescription for success.

10. **Motivation of the individual**
Early management theorists suggested a simple relationship between motivation and job satisfaction, based on the assumption that man was a rational economic being who worked for an economic reward and the more he was paid therefore the better he would work. Reward is obviously important but so are other factors. Hunt (1986) has suggested that each individual has their own goal profile which varies through the stages of life and while sometimes money may be the most significant reward, at other times

recognition may be of greater significance. An individual's orientation to work is formed by a multiplicity of factors, including their expectations which are shaped by their education, the influence of their family and the society in which they live.

11. The social needs of the individual in the workplace

The human relations school established that personal performance was affected by the people with whom the individual worked, the attitudes and the group norms established; they emphasized the social needs that people seek to satisfy in the workplace. Empirical research has established a good deal about human behaviour in the work situation since then and a brief review of some of their findings is appropriate.

12. Motivational theories

Maslow (1987) suggested that people's needs form a hierarchy through which the individual moves. At the bottom are physiological needs: shelter, warmth and food. When these are satisfied the individual looks for safety and security, then, moving upwards through love, esteem and at the top of the hierarchy, self-actualization. The theory has been difficult to prove empirically but has provided a basis for further development. Aldefer (1972) modified Maslow's model to include three levels of needs: existence needs, related needs and growth needs. Herzberg (1966) argued that there are two sets of factors affecting people. Among the hygiene factors he included salaries, working conditions, company policies, supervision and relationships with others while not satisfiers in themselves, if they are *not* present they cause dissatisfaction. Among the motivators, the factors which satisfy people, he included achievement, recognition, responsibility, growth and advancement. McClelland (1976) identified three sources of motivation: the need for affiliation, the need for power and the need for achievement.

13. Models of expectation

The work of Vroom (1964) and Porter and Lawler (1968) concentrates on identifying the relationship between the factors affecting motivation and developed models based on people's expectations of what the outcome of certain actions will be. None of the theories or models produced are comprehensive in themselves but the manager needs to be aware of them, not only because they highlight the complexity of human behaviour, but also because each gives a different perspective on how an individual may behave in the work situation.

14. McGregor's X/Y theory
   McGregor (1964) suggested two approaches to classifying people in organizations based on different and entirely opposing assumptions. *Theory X* assumes that the average person is lazy, lacks ambition, resists change and dislikes responsibility. *Theory Y* assumes that the average person is ambitious, wants responsibility and wants a job which will enable them to achieve their own goals and satisfy their ambitions. The way in which jobs are designed and the organization structured will reflect management's basic assumptions about the nature of the individual.

15. The challenge of motivation in the tourism industry
   Motivational theories are particularly significant for managers in the tourism industry which traditionally employs a large number of relatively unskilled and low-paid workers and yet whose interaction with the customer is of prime importance. This is a conundrum for the industry and an issue that needs addressing. Disney has long been admired for its ability to instil its culture and objectives in its workers and ensure that they offer a quality service. The company has attributed its success to the careful selection of people with the right personality, creative teamwork, a policy of offering rapid career advancement through the organization and training. (Fortune 1988, quoted in Murdick (1990) *et al.*)

16. The importance of training
   The increasing importance of training is recognized widely in the tourism industry in the UK and has been stressed by the BTA and the ETB in recent years. A 1992 report by NEDC emphasizes the clear benefits of training: 'There is a virtuous circle of achievement, through investment in staff training and in management skills which then permits more investment in training to give more productivity, all of which holds out the promise of greater rewards for both the enterprise and its employees.' It goes on to emphasize how the industry needs to develop a 'training culture', seeing the need to develop a multi-skilled workforce and to provide training in the systematic management and monitoring of manpower productivity. Effective training needs:

(a) clear objectives set at the outset: is the training intended to be job specific or for general staff development ?

(b) to be in an appropriate form, fitted to the needs and ability of the learner;

(c) to offer practice in the skills or knowledge required so that the fundamentals are fully grasped and instilled;

(d) to give feedback to those involved in the learning process so that they have a sense of accomplishment and progress and at the same time perceive future development needs;

(e) to assess the competences acquired as a feedback on training effectiveness as well as staff progress.

17. Customer care training

The emphasis in the industry has recently been on customer care training, designed to give businesses a competitive edge over their competitors and reduce the burden on management arising out of customer and staff dissatisfaction. A customer care training programme needs to involve all staff. In order to work, managers and frontline staff have to be committed. Such a programme should include general customer care, interpersonal and communication skills in the context of group work, techniques and strategies for dealing with problem customers and effective telephone techniques. Its essential message should be to put people first and it is worth noting that in the Disneyland visitor care programme *all* staff, including the road sweepers spend 10 days in an induction programme that focuses on making the visitor feel special.

18. Planning a customer care package

A basic customer care training package should include as a minimum:

(a) the definition of 'service' and the role of staff attitudes, welcome and care;

(b) verbal and non-verbal behaviour. Conscious and unconscious impression creation;

(c) bad service and good service – an examination of what is involved;

(d) problem customers – techniques and strategies for dealing with them.

Syndicate work under the guidance of a skilled trainer is invaluable in this area since it is important that staff see themselves as others see them and learn to treat others as they would like to be treated themselves. Poor standards in training can have a backlash effect that is extremely difficult to mitigate.

19. The link between motivation and training

The motivational impact of such training programmes should be carefully thought through. Training can facilitate staff to grow in competence, confidence and commitment. It is not merely skills enhancement but should be seen as an empowering device that reinforces culture and offers vision. It also increases job satisfaction.

20. Appraisal systems

Staff appraisal offer an opportunity for the evaluation of performance. Appraisal, whether in a management by objectives (MBO) scheme or a competency-based scheme measures the performance of the individual against the goals or standards that have been set. Managerial performance involves a complex set of activities and, therefore, presents particularly difficult measurement problems. Appraisal criteria should be as clearly and objectively identified as possible so that appraisal can play a key role:

(a) in redefining goals or objectives
(b) clarifying purpose
(c) building commitment to a sense of corporate identity.

Appraisal may be carried out on a continuous monitoring basis or though periodic reviews at set intervals, often annually. There is some dispute as to whether appraisal should be linked to reward systems.

21. Reward systems

All organizations have a system of rewards which may be classified as *extrinsic* – that is, money and perquisites which have a monetary value such as cars; and *intrinsic* – approval and recognition. Economic rewards may be used to attract, motivate and retain staff if they are used in such a way as to decrease staff turnover, improve performance and secure commitment to the organization. Though financial remuneration remains a matter of importance to most employees, the extent to which it is a direct motivational force is controversial since the evidence is mixed. Its use as a motivational device will depend on conditions in the labour market and on staff attitudes. Financial incentives may be presented as:

(a) an increase in the flat rate;
(b) a merit rate based on assessed performance;
(c) an output related bonus, e.g. increase in sales;
(d) a return for productivity improvements via changes in working practices or methods;
(e) profit-sharing.

To be effective incentives need to be related to real achievements that are seen to be objectively assessed. Productivity and output can be difficult to relate directly to staff inputs. Schemes for profit-sharing have often disappointed their instigators by not effecting the greater commitment intended. However, for senior management, sharing the risks and profits seems to have provided incentive for entrepreneurial activity. Some of the successful Queens Moat leisure developments have been undertaken under franchise arrangements that have provided a real incentive to the managers involved. There continue to be real problems facing the tourism industry however, since its image is poor and it 'retains its traditional reputation for low pay, long hours and minimal training' (NEDC 1992)

22. The future role of human resource management

Management and staff development provide the key to the future and a successful human resource management policy in any business, large or small, will seek high performance from its managers and staff. Human resource management must be viewed as an integral part of management and not isolated in an under-rated personnel function as it has tended to be historically. Treating human resources with respect and finding new and innovative ways of releasing people's abilities and talents within the organizational framework through training and development programmes is the immense management challenge facing the tourism industry. It will require a positive and determined response on the part of management and owners.

Progress test 8

For students

S1. What is meant by human resource management and why is it so important in the tourism industry? **(1, 2, 3)**

S2. What is manpower planning and why is it important? **(4)**

S3. For what purpose are job descriptions and people specifications used? **(6)**

S4. Set out an appropriate induction programme for a tourism facility known to you. **(8)**

S5. Why is an understanding of motivation so important to a manager in the tourism industry? **(12, 13, 14, 15)**

S6. What aspects should be included in an effective training programme for an admission ticket salesperson? **(16, 17)**

S7. Should appraisal systems be linked to pay? **(20, 21)**

S8. Set out in the form of a management report the arguments for making the human resource function a central pivot in any tourism attraction. **(1–22)**

For managers and practitioners

M1. Assess the degree of importance given to the human resource function in your organization. Is the balance correct in your opinion? Set out arguments to justify your response. **(1, 2, 3)**

M2. Is manpower planning undertaken in your organization? Give reasons to explain your answer. **(4)**

M3. Are accurate job descriptions and specifications used in your organisation at recruitment? **(7)**

M4. Examine the induction programmes for new staff used by your organization. Assess their effectiveness. **(8)**

M5. What training programmes are used in your organization? Assess their contribution to motivating staff and reinforcing culture. **(16, 17, 18)**

M6. What sort of appraisal system is used in your organization? Is it linked to performance related pay? **(20)**

M7. Is the human resource function a central pivot in your organization? Compare your organization's policy to that of your closest competitor. **(1–22)**

M8. Write a report, for presentation to senior managers in your organization, detailing the rationale for making human resource management a central strategic focus in the search for competitive advantage. **(1–22)**

9
Financial resource management

1. **The importance of financial management**
    Management of its financial resources is a matter of key importance to every organization regardless of its size, structure, ownership or corporate form. Many businesses with innovative and enterprising ideas, popular with their customers, have found themselves in real trouble through the failure to manage their finances or cash flow. A sound financial base facilitates and allows a business to meet its overall objectives. The significance of these issues within a profit-orientated concern is evident since shareholders or other stakeholders expect to see a return on their investment. But it is also relevant to non-profit-making organizations since the management of internal funds in particular will have a direct and immediate impact on their effectiveness and performance.

2. **Defining financial functions**
    The financial functions undertaken by an enterprise can for analytical purposes be distinguished as three separate but overlapping areas (*see* Figure 9.1).
    The financial activity reviewed under these headings is intrinsic to all organizations: capital must be procured, used effectively, monitored and the results recorded.

3. **Financial management**
    This is concerned with determining and finding appropriate sources and types of capital to fund the organization's operations and ensuring that those operations generate sufficient revenue to cover the cost of the capital. Businesses aim to raise capital on the 'best' available terms, best being a question of balancing the risk, availability and constraints against the cost. Internal needs and external opportunities have to be matched and balanced. Historically, tourism enterprises have been regarded by investors as high-risk ventures. In part, this reflects the fact that in many sectors of the industry activity necessitates capital intensive operations,

Figure 9.1 *The components of financial resource management*

while demand is perceived to be at best, variable and at worst, volatile. In the transport sector the cost of new aircraft for airlines is very high, and in the accommodation sector hotel development inevitably incurs high fixed costs. New attractions such as theme parks, for example the recently opened Euro Disney Resort, require a very large initial capital investment programme. It is rarely possible to use an incremental approach as demand builds up. On the other hand there are also examples, though few, where the initial investment is not excessive, for example on rural farm tourism developments, where existing assets can be modified for alternative use. Whatever the size of the capital investment the same principles underlie the choice of funding.

4.   Sources of finance

A business can fund its development from internal or external sources. *Internal funds* are owners' capital or previously earned profits retained within the business. The owners of many small businesses rely on internal funding, and are reluctant to look for funds outside fearing that the dilution of ownership may diminish their control of the business. For all organizations, whatever their size, ploughed back profits enhance the value of the business. Existing shareholders may well be willing to accept capital appreciation rather than income and so be satisfied with smaller dividends in the short term until the ploughed back profits generate further rewards. It is unlikely, however, that retained profits will be adequate for all expansionary developments, particularly given the capital-intensive nature of many projects, and to rely on them alone as a source of funds will undoubtedly restrict the expansion of many businesses. Nor should internal funds be regarded as costless: they have an opportunity cost which is the reward (interest) foregone by not using them elsewhere within the organization or externally. Most companies raise funds externally at some stage in their existence.

5. Raising external finance
The cost of raising finance externally will depend on a number of factors, chiefly the rate of interest generally obtaining at the time of borrowing (base rate); the length of the borrowing term; the size, security and history of the organization; its existing capital structure; managerial expertise and future prospects for the industry and/or the sector, as perceived by the potential lenders. Sometimes it is not merely the cost of borrowing that is at issue but also the availability of funds (i.e. the willingness of investors to tie up their resources over time). This will reflect the current economic climate, the attitudes of institutional lenders, tax concessions to private investors (or lack of such) or a variety of other restrictive constraints that may inhibit lending in general or lending to specific projects. Organizations therefore have to assess the financial opportunities against their own financial status and situation, the purpose for which funds are being sought and their ability to meet the costs of borrowing. A variety of options will certainly be available inside the long, medium and short-term classification that is normally used to categorize options.

6. Long-term finance
This may come from:

(a) *Equity (ordinary) shares* – shareholders provide permanent capital and are the owners and risk bearers of the business. They are rewarded by dividend payments out of profits and the capital appreciation of their investment. New equity capital can be raised in a variety of ways: by rights issues, by issue by prospectus, by an offer for sale, by a placing of shares (for example, with the large institutional shareholders – insurance companies, pension funds and so on), by issue by tender. Some 7,000 securities are listed on the London Stock Exchange which provides a marketplace for their trading. However, because of the cost of a obtaining a quotation on the Exchange, and the documentation and information requirements imposed by the Exchange (for the protection of investors and its own market status) listing is limited in the main to large and well-established companies. For them, the increasing integration of the world's financial markets and institutions have brought access to international funding, through such mechanisms as the Eurocurrency market. Increasing financial globalization has meant that large companies with international operations now have their shares quoted on the stock exchanges of the major international financial centres – London, Paris, New York and Tokyo – rather than only in the country of origin.

Example

To build its new theme park near Paris (which opened in April 1992) the US Disney corporation created a new subsidiary company, Euro Disney, and in 1989 sold a 51 per cent stake in it to institutions and private shareholders through the European stock markets, raising in all some £580 million.

Companies that have been trading for three years (as opposed to the five-year minimum required by the Stock Exchange) can if accepted use the Unlisted Securities Market (USM) as a run-in towards obtaining a full quotation. In 1987 a third market was established to provide for newer companies – only one year's audited accounts were required – but it closed in 1991. Recently, over the counter (OTC) markets have been developed for non-quoted shares. These are run by licensed share dealers so that newly formed and unquoted companies can offer their shares to investors who are prepared to take a higher risk. For most large companies, equity capital is regarded as a low-cost long-term source of capital and has been the preferred choice for funding major new investment. New equity usually increases the status and creditworthiness of the company, there is no set date for repayment and, if in the future the company needs to retain more of its earnings, dividends can be more easily varied than interest payments.

(b) *Preference shares* – which offer the holder an entitlement to payment before the ordinary shareholder, have been a favoured way of raising new capital. They have also been used as a way of increasing outside investment without losing control since they have often been offered without voting rights. Changes in UK taxation have meant that they are no longer a popular source of finance however, except in high-risk or speculative circumstances.

(c) *Debentures* – represent fixed-interest loans, usually for a fixed term, secured against assets and therefore allowable as a cost before profits are calculated for tax purposes. They provide a source of capital that businesses seek to use, providing they have sufficient asset backing and a stable profit record, to cover the annual interest payments. They may be secured or unsecured.

(d) *Loans* – Banks, insurance companies and other financial institutions offer loans secured by a mortgage or another form of charge on assets. Large or longer term borrowing is unlikely to be available unless some form of security is offered. Unsecured loans, usually short or medium term, may be available but are likely to carry a higher rate of interest. Interest payments, however, are tax-deductible. Overdrafts are usually regarded as a short-term expedient and while the interest is paid on the amount outstanding it is subject to market rate changes.

Small businesses, whether companies or partnerships, may have to choose between retained earnings or loan capital. Even medium-sized companies may prefer to borrow, because a loan means that there is no dilution of the equity and associated control; it is a fixed cost and there are tax advantages.

7. Other sources of funding
These include:

(a) *Leasing* – an increasingly popular way of reducing the large capital cost of assets such as aeroplanes, ships, buildings and property. It is also used for the acquisition of vehicles and equipment. Sale and leaseback of a hotel, for example, may help to avoid large amounts of capital being tied up and will release the funds required for further expansion. Figures from the Equipment Leasing Association (which exclude property) illustrate the growth of leasing. In 1977, UK investment in leased equipment represented some 5 per cent of all investment. By 1987, the figure had increased to nearly 18 per cent.

(b) *Factoring* and *invoice discounting* for large companies, can provide a means of releasing funds otherwise tied up in debts. When a company factors its debts it sells them at a discount which covers the servicing, financing and legal charges and the risk element to an agency which specializes in debt collection. Discounting invoices secures a cash payment in the short term but the company retains its debts and the responsibility for collecting them.

(c) *Hire purchase*, because of its ready availability, is frequently used by smaller concerns who may be finding alternative sources of funding problematic.

8. Capital structure

Capital structure is the balance between loan (debt) and share (equity) capital and is referred to as *gearing* (9:19). It has to be carefully planned to provide appropriate risk/reward ratios for investors, and to minimize capital costs for the business. A company's choice of capital structure should, therefore, reflect its view of:

(a) its own ability to earn in the future and to pay out dividends and/or interest payments as well as finance future investments
(b) the risk of borrowing and the cost of that borrowing on its profits. It should at the same time relate its own position to
(c) the capital structure prevailing in the industry and
(d) the risk factor in the industry as a whole, as seen by investors and institutions.

Any new developments that alter the balance must be given careful consideration since they will also affect the investors' view of the company.

9. Management Buy-Outs

Management Buyouts (MBOs) represent a different approach to the financing of an enterprise. Developed in the 1970s and 1980s as a solution to the problem of a declining manufacturing sector, they spread in the late 1980s into the service industries. In 1989 more than 500 MBOs were recorded.They have become chiefly associated in the UK with the divestment of a subsidiary or a part of a business that no longer fits with the portfolio or the strategy of a large conglomerate, as for example the MBO of Wookey Hole from Pearson plc. The development of institutional financial arrangements, allowing debt-financed equity deals, has facilitated and even encouraged the process.

In most MBOs, members of the management team acquire equity and so have a direct interest in the future performance of the unit they have bought. If the senior managers' purchase of equity has been financed by debt, as is usually the case, the need to service interest charges, together with the desire to maintain ownership and control, provides a strong incentive to increase profitability. Two other aspects are relevant: a successful management buy-out, in creating a small organization, may well reduce the bureaucratic controls and systems pervasive in large organizations while at the same time increasing the flexibility and the ability to respond to consumer needs. This may well be enhanced if share ownership is not restricted to a small group of senior managers but extended to other employees at all levels. Increasingly MBOs are to be found in the contracting out of local authority services, for example, leisure and sport complexes.

10. Local authority financing

There are, in the tourism industry, a number of facilities which are either wholly, or in part, financed by local authorities and which do not have the same degree of control over their funding as companies in the private sector. The amount of finance to be made available from such sources may vary from year to year, making planning and investment decisions more difficult for managers in such organizations. Beamish Open Air Museum has been partially funded by local authorities since it was first established 20 years ago. The proportion of income provided by the local authorities was much higher in the early years and has been reduced progressively as the museum started to finance itself out of earnings. Over an 18 year period an average of 50 per cent of Beamish's income was provided by local authorities but this ranged from nearly 85 per cent in 1971–2 to only 18 per cent in 1988–9 (Johnson and Turner 1992). Attractions in the public sector also receive funding from bodies such as the tourist boards or English Heritage. Historically, grants have been an important source of finance for the industry, but they are now more difficult to obtain. Sponsorship from commercial organizations is another source of financial support. Overall mixed funding of this type creates different constraints for the managers concerned with the organization's financial resources and decision-making about its future.

Example : The National Trust ————————————————

Any ordinary commercial enterprise with rising income and assets valued at more than £2 billion would offer its financial director considerable freedom and flexibility for strategic development. In reality the National Trust's finance director, however 'has to contend with unique management problems. He has no discretion over how sizeable amounts of his cash may be spent and his assets ... are worthless as collateral.' He said, 'In trying to preserve things forever you discover that what would be perceived as an asset in the ordinary commercial world cannot be sold. In financial terms it becomes a liability' (*Financial Times*, 25.10.89).

The Trust's funds of some £200 million are made up of bequests and donations which cannot be spent for general purposes. A capital endowment fund of £110 million has to be kept intact in order to generate income.

In 1991 the Trust's income was nearly £80 million, made up as follows:

membership	43 per cent
property income	27 per cent
investment income	21 per cent
enterprises (shops etc.)	7 per cent
gifts	2 per cent

A further £20 million was drawn from various funds of the Trust so that income and expenditure could balance. (*National Trust Annual Report 1991*).

---

11. Management accounting

Management accounting is as important for subsidized businesses as it is in the wholly commercial organization. If managers are to ensure that financial resources are allocated efficiently within the organization, they need information to plan and control their use and this is provided by the use of management accounting systems and techniques. Information on costs, turnover, profits and cash flows are vital for management decision-making.

12. Cost accounting

Analysis and allocation of costs is essential so that managers are aware of what their activities cost in each period of time. Costs can be categorized in two main ways: variable and fixed. Many direct costs are variable in the sense that they fluctuate with the level of service provided. Businesses incur *direct costs*, that is, those which can be directly attributed to a service (such as raw materials or wages) and *fixed* or *overhead costs*, that is, those arising from running the business generally and which have to be apportioned in an equitable fashion between the various parts of the business. Fixed costs such as rents and interest payments have to be met regardless of revenue generated. In the service industries generally, salary and wage bills make up a large part of costs. That part of the wages and salaries bill which is for permanent staff may be regarded as a fixed cost, while the wages of part-time and seasonal staff will form part of the variable costs of the organization. Operating and maintenance costs will be high in the transport and accommodation sectors of the tourism industry, while in the hotel and catering sector raw material costs will be higher than, for example, at a theme park. Control of costs is vital in any organization.

13. Cash flow
Management of cash flow is a vital aspect of management accounting, essential for all organizations whatever their size. A business must ensure that it has sufficient revenue coming in to meet its expenses at any one time. This may be particularly difficult in the start-up period when costs such as salaries and wages have to be met before the facility starts to generate income. There are many examples of businesses, large and small, apparently trading briskly, but failing to ensure that the cash coming in will cover the payments they have to make and, therefore, being forced into receivership and liquidation. Larger organizations with plentiful revenue flowing in can employ sophisticated, short-term money placings to generate further revenue. That is, they can use their cash flow to increase income rather than letting it sit in the bank. They must, however, monitor these movements to ensure that they have cash available when required.

14. Budgeting
The function of budgeting is to plan the allocation of resources and the control process in the business, over a period of time (*see also* Chapter 3). Budgets are an essential part of making, implementing and controlling the plans of the business. Most businesses budget on an annual basis against the background of a longer-term plan. Departments are allocated resources to meet their costs and at the same time targets are set as to what should be achieved. When integrated together budgets should achieve the objectives set for the organization as a whole. The allocation of resources by budgeting is usually based on information from previous allocations, but the practice of adding say 10 per cent to the previous year's allocation is generally condemned. Zero-budgeting, that is, starting from scratch each year in working out the costs to be met, is much recommended today. Because resources are always scarce, the process of budgeting necessarily involves negotiation and bargaining between departments. Departments seeking an increase in their budget will have to justify their need for it to the senior management, since giving to one

department almost invariably means taking away from another. Regular management accounting information on a weekly, monthly and/or quarterly basis can provide a check on budget spending, costs and the achievement of targets, thus enabling corrections to be made, rather than departments finding at the year end that they have overspent their budget.

15. Investment appraisal

This is usually one of the responsibilities given to management accountants. Investment decisions tie up substantial amounts of capital in new ventures, expansion or replacement schemes: many of the decisions are irreversible and the repercussions of the decisions have to be lived with for a long time. It is therefore imperative to approach the decision in a rational and precise manner. In this context the management accountant can calculate the cost of raising capital and evaluate the expected returns against the planned expenditure, allowing for tax concessions and/or grants if available. Various formal techniques are available: computerized packages are available to assist calculations. *Discounted cash flows* (internal rates of return or Net Present Value) are technically correct but many organizations still use simpler, if rather primitive, payback or average profit calculations. All these methods are based on forecasts of future net incomes and costs. In volatile industries such forecasts are notoriously difficult to make and the inherent uncertainty and risk inevitable.

16. Financial reporting

Much of the information produced by the management accounting process will be presented in the company's Report and Accounts, made up on an annual basis for the information of its shareholders and other stakeholders. This is a report by the company on its performance over the previous year and its financial position at the year end for the benefit of those who have invested in it. Some of the information all companies are required by law to present (the amount of detail legally required has increased in recent years) though most large companies in any case have favoured a move towards giving more information to all its stakeholders.

There are two principal statements presented in financial reporting:

(a) *the balance sheet* which gives a summary of the company's financial position at the end of the accounting period, balancing its assets and its liabilities; and

(b) *the profit and loss account* which shows the company's income and expenditure over a period of time.

17. Financial ratios

Deriving from these a number of ratios can be calculated which have a wider significance than the absolute figures on their own. They can be used to compare the financial performance of companies of different size as well against an average for the sector, both in that year and over a number of years in order to establish a trend; to compare, for example, hotels, airlines or tourist attractions of a certain type. They will also be used over a period of time to establish the organization's financial status, since they offer some measurement of its efficiency, profitability, liquidity and credit-worthiness.

18. Return on capital employed (ROCE)

ROCE assesses overall profitability and efficiency and is one of the most widely used evaluation technique. It is calculated as:

Profit before interest and tax ÷ capital employed
(where capital employed = fixed assets + working capital
i.e. cash, stocks and debtors).

Problems with valuations of capital assets and the calculation of representative profit figures can lead to distortions, but as an indicator of financial efficiency this is widely used.

19. Gearing

Gearing is the term used when measuring the proportion of assets funded by interest-bearing borrowing compared with the proportion of assets funded by the shareholders. It is calculated as:

net debt (i.e. borrowings − cash) ÷ shareholders equity
(i.e. share capital, reserves and minority interests).

A high gearing ratio indicates a higher level of risk but a greater potential gain to the shareholder. Over the 1980s, as the balance between equity and debt changed, much higher gearing ratios became common and acceptable to the investing institutions.

The repercussions of this trend have been interesting to observe during the recession when high interest rates, in conjunction with declining revenue, have given major problems to highly geared companies. Many have been forced into the sale of assets. Takeovers and bankruptcies have also occurred.

20. Interest cover ratio

This shows the number of times the profit earned by the business (before interest and tax) is greater than the interest charges it has to meet.

21. Dividend cover ratio

This shows the number of times the business could pay its dividend out of its earnings.

22. Earnings per share

This is calculated by taking profit (after tax and minority interests, but before extraordinary items) and dividing it by the total number of the company's shares. It is used principally as a comparative profitability ratio.

23. The prices/earnings (P/E) ratio

The P/E ratio is calculated by dividing the market price of the ordinary shares by earnings per share.

24. Dividend yield

This is calculated by dividing the dividend per share by the market price of the share.

25. The liquidity ratio

This is calculated by dividing current assets by current liabilities to show the extent to which the company's liabilities are covered by its assets.

26. Other ratios

There are other ratios – *profit margin* and *asset turnover* for example – as well as those concerning stocks and debts, which may be calculated to provide greater detail about any company's financial position.

27. Financial management in context

In summary, managing the financial resources of the

organization in the most efficient and effective way requires a constant flow of information and the deployment of considerable skills in interpreting and using that information for decision-making.

Progress test 9

For students

S1. Why is financial management important to both private sector and non-profit making organizations? **(1)**

S2. Select a private sector organization in the tourism industry and identify the main sources of finance by examining the company accounts. Explain the probable rationale behind its capital structure. **(4, 6, 7, 10)**

S3. Why is cash flow so important? Can a company be profitable and still experience liquidity problems? **(1, 13)**

S4. Explain the way costs may be categorized. Why are such distinctions useful? **(12)**

S5. What is budgeting? Why is it necessary? **(14)**

S6. What aspects of an organization's activity does financial reporting cover? Who is interested in this information and why? **(16)**

S7. Explain what is meant by gearing? Rank the following concerns for what you might expect to be increasing gearing ratios: **(19)**

(a) an hotel in city centre
(b) an airline company
(c) a caravan site
(d) a rural bygones museum on an owner occupied farm
(e) an electronic games centre at a seaside resort in leased buildings.

S8. Set out the major ratios used to appraise the financial performance of organizations. **(20–6)**

For managers and practitioners

M1. What is the relevance of financial management to your organization? **(1, 3)**

M2. Set out the capital structure of your organization and explain your findings. What changes have occurred over its history? **(4–7)**

M3. Compare your answer for question 2 with the capital structure of one or more other companies in the industry. Identify and explain the differences and similarities that you observe. **(4–7)**

M4. Why is it important to monitor cash flow in all organizations? What procedures are used for this purpose in your organization? **(13)**

M5. What cost information is collected and analyzed in your organization? **(12)**

M6. How is the budgeting process undertaken in your organization? Who sets targets and who does the monitoring? **(14)**

M7. Examine the information contained in your organization's latest financial report. At a personal level assess the extent to which this may be regarded as a public relations exercise.

M8. What are the major ratios used in your organization to assess its financial performance? **(17–26)**

10

Operations management

1. Introduction

Operations management is concerned with the design, operation and control of the 'system' that matches the organization's resources to customer service needs. All organizations need systems to transform their resources (inputs) into the services (outputs) demanded by customers. This systems activity can be most usefully described and understood as a transformation process, as set out in Fig. 10.1. As the transformation process takes place, value is added.

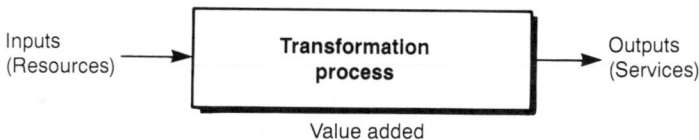

```
Inputs                 ┌──────────────────────┐              Outputs
(Resources)   ───────▶ │  Transformation      │ ───────▶     (Services)
                       │      process         │
                       └──────────────────────┘
                            Value added
```

Figure 10.1 *The organization's transformation process*

2. The role of the operations manager

Operations managers must link staff, equipment, materials and information about markets and technology to the actual demand patterns of customers. The central issue is to reconcile and balance customer needs and preferences within the constraints imposed by the organization's resources at any one time. In the short run this may involve optimizing the use of current capacity by rescheduling staff and/or modifying layouts and or quality standards, by altering the parameters already established within the system. In the longer term a wider range of options may be open, allowing the alteration of those parameters by the expansion or contraction of capacity, or by redesigning the system itself and the facilities it incorporates, to enable objectives to be met. Figure 10.2 sets out the stages in this process; in reality the process may not proceed in such a logically sequential fashion. Constraints of time, resources or availability of

information may be factors having an effect on the way in which
the process is carried out.

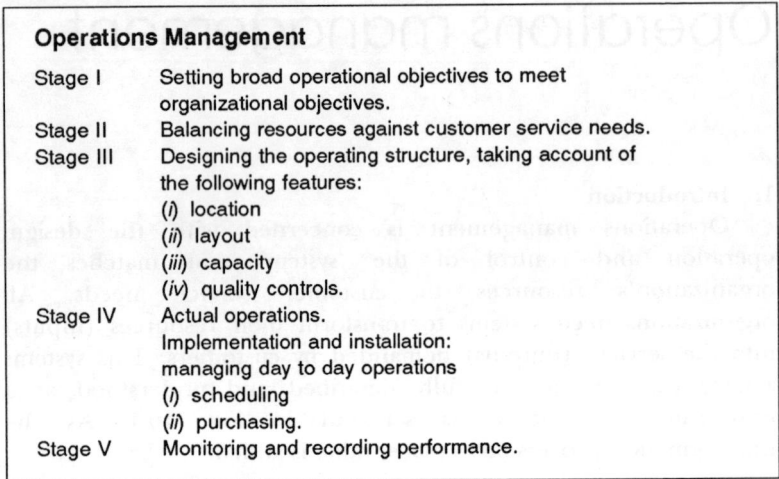

Operations Management

Stage I   Setting broad operational objectives to meet
           organizational objectives.
Stage II   Balancing resources against customer service needs.
Stage III Designing the operating structure, taking account of
           the following features:
           (*i*) location
           (*ii*) layout
           (*iii*) capacity
           (*iv*) quality controls.
Stage IV   Actual operations.
           Implementation and installation:
           managing day to day operations
           (*i*) scheduling
           (*ii*) purchasing.
Stage V   Monitoring and recording performance.

Figure 10.2 *The decision making process for operation management*

3.

The decision making and problem solving involved in this
process may be complex and will require a range of knowledge,
skills and techniques. Although this would be expected in large
organizations, the same principles will apply even in small units
where the decision making may be undertaken by a single
individual but still be very demanding in terms of the range of skills
required. The systems chosen must be:

(a) appropriate to enable the overall objectives to be met;
(b) feasible and practical within the constraints operating;
(c) flexible and adaptable to meet changing demand patterns and
environmental influences.

4. An illustrative example
    We are all familiar with motorway service stations. They are
classic examples of operational units that provide a range of
facilities for travellers that we all take very much for granted. The
series of operational decisions that were needed to set them up
originally as well as others that are currently being taken to ensure
effective operations provide a good illustration of the operations

management process. In the first instance decisions had to be made regarding location, facilities to be provided, capacity size, layout and design in conjunction with quality of service. These are usually classed as long run decisions since once taken they are difficult to modify. In the shorter term some decisions are taken on an almost daily basis to decide on the scheduling of staff, purchasing, maintenance, cleaning and other services essential to smooth operations. Many of these decisions are complex and involve problem solving skills and knowledge unlikely to be found in one individual. Teamwork is therefore often required and activities have to be allocated to reflect experience and expertise. We will now examine some of the most crucial decisions in turn.

5. Location decisions

Location is important to all businesses since it affects cost structures in terms of rent, site values and so on. In tourism it is of paramount importance since revenue will also be responsive to the accessibility and environs of the facility's situation. Location is synonymous with availability for the tourist. Poor location is invariably difficult to offset and will always involve additional expenditure on marketing or promotion to compensate for site disadvantages. The effect on the bottom line is obvious and so it is common sense to ensure that optimum site selection procedures should be implemented, wherever possible, at the start of a new project. It is useful to distinguish between general locale decisions and specific site selection. The former involve a wide macro-type perspective; this may be at national or regional level but essentially involves establishing the geographical boundaries within which profitable operation is feasible. Site selection involves choosing specific property sites with appropriate physical or aesthetic characteristics for the development.

6. A framework for site selection

There are no hard and fast rules that can be laid down for location or site selection but a set procedure providing a framework for the decision making stages is desirable if only to avoid important issues being overlooked. The following stages of selection can be identified:

(a) *Identification of influential factors.*
  (*i*) transportation and communication networks;
  (*ii*) economic and social profiles;

(*iii*) climatic and geographical factors;
(*iv*) the local community;
(*v*) demographic factors;
(*vi*) management/staff preferences.

(b) *Weighting of factors*: (*i*) to (*vi*) inclusive, according to their importance for the particular facility or attraction.

There is, for example, little point in siting a leisure centre based on swimming facilities in a place without good public transport links, since many of its users will be children and teenagers. On the other hand, a golf course will be more likely to attract customers with their own cars but the socio-economic profile of the surrounding area will require greater weighting.

(c) *Compilation of a scoring matrix*, that is, a scale for each factor multiplied by its weight.

(d) *Selection of site based on total scores.*

7. **Specific factors for site selection**
    Specific factors influential in site selection are:

(a) transport networks;
(b) space requirements;
(c) zoning/character of environs;
(d) services available and needed;
(e) people flows/demographic analysis of catchment area;
(f) land and building costs;
(g) labour availability including the culture, skills and attitudes of staff available as well as likely competition for them.

8. **Site selection factors in context**
    In both general location and specific site selection it is important not to focus too much on the quantifiable factors such as land costs to the exclusion of the qualitative factors such as the environmental aspects of the area or region. The potential revenue impact of location decisions should always be the dominant factor.

Finally it should be noted that decisions may have to be taken under considerable time pressures, for example, the availability of the site, tender-type situations, confidentiality and planning issues. Any one of these may preclude thorough analysis.

Example: *Center Parcs Sherwood Forest: location decision* _____

Market-related criteria

Factors	Sherwood Forest
Proximity to potential market	8 million people within 2 hours' drive
Ease of access	Good
Support facilities	Towns, villages nearby
Competing facilities	None
Other tourism demand generators	Sherwood Forest itself

Physical criteria

Site aesthetics	Views, varied flora and fauna
Water supply	Center Parcs complements nature
Ability of land to support recreation	Developed man-made lake etc.

Other criteria

Manpower availability and good labour relations	Functional managers attracted from restaurants, hotels
Availability and cost of land, zoning and regulations	Land costs less than nearer to London, labour supply, 440 acres for 629 villas, 3000 people
Government financial assistance	ETB and local government assistance to £34 million investment
Socio-economic features of host area/local reaction	Local support – 400 jobs. Environment enhanced.

(*Source*: J. L. Bentley, *Center Parcs*, PAVIC Publications, 1989)

9. Delivery systems and layouts

The choice of the layout of the facility is determined by the need to deliver the service to meet customer needs within the constraints of space, time, staff and the technology available to the organization. The way in which these components are combined depends on the specific characteristics of the facility. In a theme park many issues will be relevant; for example the interplay of the individual rides within the total experience being offered will have to be considered. In contrast, a small, specialist museum can take a much simpler and more straightforward approach. At the Tower of London, visitor flows and throughput patterns were major criteria in designing the Crown Jewels display; security factors were also of major significance.

10. Deciding staff to visitor ratios

The amount of visitor/staff interaction and involvement also has to be decided. In virtually all catering and shopping units decisions have to be made as to the extent self-service will be integrated into the layout. Decision makers in charge of historic houses have to decide whether visitors should be guided around in escorted and therefore controlled parties or whether to allow greater freedom in time and space but accept the concomitant need for extra interpretation and enhanced security. Managers of countryside parks and nature reserves have to decide on the extent of supervised facilities and whether a resident warden is required. Minimizing labour costs invariably increases the required capital investment and leads to a trade-off between long-term investment needs and short-term expenditure.

11. Designing and managing the layout

In all facilities the following factors require consideration when designing and managing the layout:

(a) *aesthetic factors* – the creation of ambience and image;
(b) *customer flows* – to maximize throughout without giving the impression of congestion or making customers feel they are being hurried;
(c) *ergonomics* – the relationship of staff to equipment in order to minimize costs and optimize the use of labour in creating an attractive customer environment. Reception areas in recently developed leisure centres reflect how these may be achieved;
(d) *versatility* and *flexibility* – layouts must be planned to allow for fluctuations in demand in the short term and as far as possible in the long term – consider food areas in retail and leisure centres which use separate islands that can be minimally manned at slack times but brought into full use quickly at peak times.

12. Capacity planning

Tourist demand, as we have seen, fluctuates on an hourly, daily, weekly and seasonal basis, but the service has to be delivered when demanded. A crucial decision has to be made at start-up about optimal capacity and its relation to demand levels. For some organizations there are additional constraints on their capacity imposed by legislation or regulatory requirements.

Example: **British Airports Authority** _____

Privatized in 1987, BAA plc owns, manages and runs Heathrow, Gatwick and Stansted airports in England, and the Scottish airports. About half its income comes from airport charges (landing fees, aircraft parking fees and a levy on departing passengers) and the other half from retailing (duty and tax free shops), car parking and other charges associated with airline accommodation such as the rental of check-in and ticket desks, lounges and freight sheds.

Major factors determining capacity:

    (a) Runway slots
    (b) Aircraft stand and parking availability
    (c) Check-in facilities
    (d) Baggage reclaim facilities
    (e) Security screening
    (f) Customs capacity
    (g) Immigration check-ins.

Tourists have to be handled at BAA's airports along with other travellers and on behalf of a number of airlines (70 use Heathrow, one of the busiest airports in the world) and while **(e)**, **(f)** and **(g)** of the factors listed above are government requirements there are also constraints imposed by the Aviation Security Act.

_____

Significant questions for management to ask themselves at an early stage in capacity planning are:

(a) How much spare capacity are we prepared (i.e. can we afford) to carry during slower periods? This is particularly difficult when public holiday periods are under review.
(b) How serious would be the negative impact of failing to meet demand at peak periods?
(c) If we build in excess capacity, how expensive will it be to maintain in terms of fixed and running costs?
(d) Could we use strategic devices to shift demand patterns, for example, by special pricing or promotion campaigns?

13. Scheduling and capacity utilization

Unless excess capacity is to be deliberately maintained at all times, regardless of expense, scheduling and queue management will have to be undertaken by management. Analytical models can be used to help in this decision making:

(a) Increasingly, computer-aided simulation modelling is used to determine optimal capacity: forecasts of demand patterns and the variability of arrival times, the length of service time, customer expectations and behaviours and so on, can be incorporated in models to predict the queue lengths associated with alternative capacity levels or alternative layout facilities.

(b) Queueing analysis can be used to determine optimal scheduling of service units and manning to meet customer service needs and to plan anticipated variations in the short term.

(c) Queue management then has to be planned and implemented. The queuing channels may be single, multiple or parallel: service stages may be arranged in different formats and rules for queue discipline have to be established. For example, customers may be segregated according to priority ratings.

14. The psychology of waiting

All scheduling and queuing management decisions involve, in essence, trade-offs between costs and queue length. Appreciating customer attitudes to time spent queuing is crucial; the experience of waiting has to be assessed, not from a management perspective but from the viewpoint of the customer. Expectations and perceptions are extremely important in this context. An excellent review of the psychology of waiting has been written by D.H. Maister (in Lovelock 1988, p. 176). The main propositions are summarized below:

(a) unoccupied time feels longer than occupied time
(b) pre-process waits feel longer than in-process waits
(c) anxiety makes waits seem longer
(d) uncertain waits are longer than known waits
(e) unexplained waits are longer than explained waits
(f) unfair waits are longer than equitable waits
(g) the more valuable the service the longer the customer will wait
(h) solo waits feel longer than group waits.

15. Creative queuing devices

These propositions can be applied in any tourism facility management situation where queuing occurs. They can be adapted to minimize the frustration and boredom that results if customers become aware of time slipping by. Some examples will illustrate:

*Example : Jorvik*_____

Since it was opened in 1984 Heritage Project's Jorvik in York has attracted long queues because of the popularity of the time cars, the use of which, however, imposes an inflexible restraint on throughput. Buskers and street entertainers have been encouraged to perform to amuse the crowds queuing around the courtyard. Noticeboards at intervals inform those waiting how long it will be before they are admitted. Thus **(a)**, **(c)**, **(d)**, **(e)** and **(g)** of the propositions above are met. Similarly at Madame Tussaud's, a highly popular attraction where substantial queues build up, boards above the queue confront visitors with questions that act as catalysts for group discussion or personal thought. The answers are provided retrospectively as the queue moves forward – an informative and time diversion role combined.

---

*Example : Alton Towers*_____

Inside the theme park all rides are free, inevitably leading to queues at busy times. Queues for the prestigious major rides are longer than those for the less dramatic experiences. Again entertainers are used to amuse those queuing, who are also given some indication of the likely length of their wait. Queues are segmented so that the process appears shorter and after entry to some of the buildings leading to the rides, participants feel they are now part of the process and can watch videos that surround the queuing area. Barriers keep the queues orderly and equitable and snake patterns are used so that groups form – and chat – making the time pass more quickly. Numbers **(a)**, **(b)**, **(d)** and **(e)** of the propositions are met again.

---

16. **Levels of service/quality**

These will be based on the marketing focus that has been adopted, reflecting the strategic marketing policy decisions already taken (*see* Chapters 6 and 7).

17. **Purchasing**

Purchasing decisions are operational matters now recognized as important determinants of the profit levels achieved. Not only do they directly affect profits through costs but they impact on quality control. Operations managers must address issues such as balancing availability and least cost, reliability and risk. Increasingly Just-In-Time (JIT) mechanisms are being used and aided by computerized stock control and order systems. Centralized buying, with the concentration of expertise and bargaining power has to be set against the flexibility and responsiveness of decentralized systems.

18. Installing a purchasing system
A purchasing system will need to be installed allowing for information gathering under the following heads:

(a) specifications;
(b) supplier identification;
(c) tender/bid;
(d) orders;
(e) deliveries;
(f) checking;
(g) payments; and
(h) appraisal.

19. Maintenance and servicing
Equipment and facilities need to be maintained in good working order. Decisions will need to be taken as to whether maintenance is to be undertaken in-house or by use of agents. Time schedules for maximizing reliability and minimizing disruption will need to be worked out. This is an important aspect influencing the overall quality and reliability of the facility.

20. Appraising and monitoring the system
Appraisal and monitoring must be undertaken on a continuous basis to ensure quality standards are met and maintained. It is not always easy for those operating a system to recognize its defects or even to appraise its merits. Objectivity is essential – the best standards of comparison are those of competitors, whose performance should be equalled or preferably exceeded. Monitoring of competitors on a comparative basis is, therefore, essential. Customer audits carried out on a regular basis can also be used to add to the appraisal profile. In an ideal world there should be no customer complaints, but in the real world careful monitoring of the complaints that will be made which should indicate problem areas that need the attention of operations managers (*see* Chapter 11).

21. Operations management techniques
Techniques used in operations management (OR), developed for use in manufacturing production units, can usefully be

transferred, with adaptations, to the type of services provided by tourism facilities. Many of these are sophisticated and rely on the use of computers for their implementation.

22. Effective project management
Setting up new tourism projects or modifying existing ones require what is in effect project management – a major effort towards a specific end. Festivals and special events provide interesting examples to illustrate the project management approach. Increasingly such events contribute to tourism as temporary attractions that may range from the mega events (for example, the Olympics or World Fairs) to small local events (for example, Morris Dancers' rush cart festivals or the Highland games in Scotland). In all cases they are used to pull in visitors to a particular area for a specific purpose. The motivations may of course vary enormously and be planned as deliberate catalysts for development, destination renewal or to enliven static attractions or areas. Regardless of their size or duration such projects require:

(a) *Planning*
   (*i*)   goals
   (*ii*) time and cost estimates
   (*iii*) team building
(b) *Scheduling*
   (*i*)   resourcing
   (*ii*) sequencing activities
(c) *Controlling*
   (*i*)   monitoring
   (*ii*) revising plans and targets
(d) *Implementation* and *Operation*

23. Project management planning techniques
The techniques available to help with these stages include GANTT project planning charts, named after their originator, Henry Gantt, CPA (critical path analysis) and PERT (programme evaluation and review technique). Computerized packages are used for more complex projects, for example, in Disneyland. CPA and PERT are usually treated separately in operations management texts but they overlap and in essence are quite simple. The network analysis that both of them use represents a plan of action and priorities within that plan.

24. CPA
The critical path analysis approach sets out to:

(a) identify all the activities and tasks involved in the project;
(b) place them in an appropriate sequence, i.e. decide on precedence/follow-on etc.;
(c) apportion time-scales and network activities;
(d) calculate the critical time path through.

The information laid out can be used to plan, schedule, monitor and control the project.

25. PERT
The programme evaluation and review technique similarly breaks down projects into events and activities. In the analysis, activities are time-scheduled on the shortest possible, most probable and longest time estimates. The probability of completion dates can then be calculated. The technique is particularly useful when the project completion date is of great significance, as for example when a grand opening has to be scheduled.

Both these techniques, but PERT in particular, allow activity times to be studied and costs identified. Activity time is invariably a reflection of how many resources in terms of labour, equipment and finance are scheduled for certain purposes. The analysis clarifies the options open to management and in some cases, where the critical path is extended because of one activity, it may prove to be worth increasing the resource allocation to that activity to shorten the overall project completion time. In the mid-1980s British Airways used PERT to plan the introduction of its new corporate image and identity, as expressed in the fittings of its aircraft, staff uniforms, vehicles, shops and check-in desks.

26. Graphic charting
Graphic charting can be used to present visually complex and interrelated information, such as, flow processes, operator activities, activity/performance charts and quality control over time and on a relative basis.

27. Linear programming
Linear programming is a mathematical technique, particularly useful at the planning stage when managers need to make decisions regarding resource usage, for example, manpower planning in large

organizations. The basis of the technique is that at least in the short term many resources are constrained, but within those constraints the organization seeks to maximize its profit, or its efficiency, and minimize its use of resources or its costs. Linear programming will identify the alternative ways of doing so, either graphically where the analysis is limited to two variables, or via a computer programme when more variables can be introduced into the equation.

28. The tools of management

Two significant points arise from this discussion of the techniques available for managers to use:

(a) These are *management tools* and should be used as such; they are no substitute for managerial experience and expertise.
(b) They exemplify the use of computer software and information technology in the industry as a whole.

29. Information Technology (IT)

IT now permeates the whole array of tourism facilities. It has high visibility in transportation where computerized reservation systems are a prominent feature of daily activity and in other areas where booking systems are used. It has less visibility, but extremely significant implications, in areas such as security, where electronic sensing equipment and transmission of information to central points permit supervision at a previously unanticipated level, without an army of personnel. Its use in interpretation has allowed an array of imaginative and ingenious displays incorporating visual and aural stimulation.

30. Visual impacts

Even the smallest attraction needs to present information to the visitor. The first contact between the visitor and the facility may be made through a brochure or an advertisement before the visitor arrives at the facility; this will create certain expectations which the facility will either meet or disappoint. At the very minimum, signing will be required at the facility. The visual impact of signs on the visitors will influence their 'perception' of the attraction, its image and the quality of the experience they will be offered. Signs therefore need to be effective, clear and appropriate in terms of their location and number. As well as being purely functional they can, by their colour, typology and design enhance visitor experience and play a part in conveying the spirit of the attraction.

31. Interpretation techniques

For most attractions, further interpretation is necessary to aid visitor understanding and enhance enjoyment. Increasingly, attractions use audio-visual displays, demonstrations and information processed in some way by the use of information technology. Over the last decade interpretation has become an art in itself; it requires information, technical expertise and specialized knowledge. The use of animation in theme parks and heritage centres throughout the world has shown how technology via animatronics can be used as entertainment for 'reviving' dinosaurs, Queen Victoria or pop stars.

32. Effective data processing

At a more prosaic level, information technology allows the rapid and accurate processing of data for accounting and control purposes. Again, this has real implications for the process of operations management. An example of its application would be in the area of purchasing. Historically, manual stock control formed the basis of purchasing policies; decisions regarding economic order quantities and so on, were calculated and orders placed, on a manual basis. IT now permits ongoing modelling of stock situations, direct contacts with suppliers so that 'just-in-time' (JIT) ordering can be utilized to keep storage, administrative and other costs at a minimum. Specifications and suppliers records, orders, deliveries and checking can be regularly monitored.

33. Tourist information centres

Tourist information centres (TICs) are increasingly using IT as part of their service for booking and information supply. In Scotland, where the network of TICs has a long and successful history, IT is integrated into their support system. The ETB has spent a great deal of effort, energy and resources designing a large, integrated IT network for information purposes. The Wales Tourist Board has recently installed a 24-hour computerized TIC on the M4 into Wales supplying information on accommodation, attractions and events.

34. Health and safety regulations

Health and safety are an important consideration for

operational decisions both for staff and visitors. Owners have a duty to take such care as is reasonable to ensure that all visitors using, or on the premises, are safe. Substantial claims for compensation are possible if it can be proved that owners or management have been negligent in their duties. Current legislation must, therefore, be taken into account and advice sought if there is any doubt about responsibilities.

35. Integrating functional activity

In summary, operations management is at the centre of the transformation process which takes resources and, by adding value, offers the visitor to the facility a service. The operations manager must, however, integrate his activities with those of other functions, marketing and human resources management for example, in order for the organization to achieve its objectives efficiently and effectively.

Progress test 10

For students

S1. What do operations managers do? List the activities for which they are usually responsible. **(1, 2, 3)**

S2. What are the factors that have to be taken into account when deciding on the selection of a site for a tourism attraction? **(5, 6, 7)**

S3. Select two or three tourism attractions as examples and then analyze the merits and drawbacks of their location. **(5)**

S4. Why is the layout of a tourist attraction so important? **(9, 10)**

S5. Why is capacity planning so important to tourism facilities? Pay particular attention to the crucial factors that need to be taken into account when determining optimal capacity. **(11)**

S6. Using Maister's queuing propositions, analyze the extent to which they were used in a tourism facility that you have recently visited. **(14)**

S7. Discuss the extent to which service quality depends on operations staff and their motivation and attitudes. (Chapter 1:12)

S8. Are purchasing decisions significant to tourism attractions? **(17, 18)**

S9. Identify specific techniques (Operational Research) that would be useful if you were in charge of a major expansion in a tourism facility. **(21–7)**

S10. Identify the present use of information technology (IT) as a management tool in tourist facilities. How do you see this developing in the future? What are the implications of such developments? **(29–32)**

For managers and practitioners

M1. Identify the individual(s) who is (are) responsible for operations in your organization. List the activities in which they are involved and appraise their role.

M2. What factors determined the location of your facility? Assess the amount of discretion that was available regarding site selection when the initial decision was made. Set out the strengths and weaknesses of the present location and analyze the extent to which these could have been forecast when the original location decision was made. **(5–8)**

M3. To what extent has the layout of your facility been purpose-planned? Identify the crucial features that at present aid or impede effective operations. **(9–11)**

M4. Appraise from the visitors' perspective the 'design' features of your establishment and compare them with those of major competitors, highlighting areas that should be improved. **(11)**

M5. What is the total capacity of your facility? Plot this against the demand patterns/fluctuations that are experienced. Examine the extent to which excess capacity is a problem and catalogue the approaches that are currently used to offset the problem. Are there other alternatives that could be used? **(12–14)**

M6. To what extent are Maister's queuing propositions utilized in your facility? **(14, 15)**

M7. Appraise, at an operational level, how much attention is paid to 'quality of service' within your facility. Is the balance appropriate?

M8. How much managerial time and attention is allocated to purchasing decisions in your organization? In your view is this appropriate? **(17, 18)**

M9. If your facility was planning a major expansion, what operational techniques would you suggest should be employed? **(21–7)**

M10. To what extent is information technology used as a management tool in your facility? How does this compare with other similar establishments? **(29–32)**

Part five

Appraising and evaluating performance

Introduction to part five

1. Introduction

This section reviews the complex problems associated with measuring business performance and examines the concepts that can be used to underpin the exercise. Issues to be addressed include *why*, *when*, *how* and *by whom* should performance be appraised.

2. The role of the effective appraisal

Appraisal and evaluation of the *effectiveness* and the *efficiency* of organizational performance are essential for a number of reasons of which the most important are:

(a) to assess how well customer needs are being met;
(b) to measure how well the goals and objectives set by the organization have been and are being achieved;
(c) to use the feedback to define learning and training needs and to redefine goals and objectives.

3. Appraisal of organizational performance

The appraisal and evaluation process should reveal how well the individual management functions, which have been discussed in previous chapters, have integrated their operations to achieve the objectives of the organization as a whole. Appraisal of organizational performance, therefore, also acts as a control mechanism for management, providing opportunities for feedback and correction. It should ideally be carried out on a continuous basis.

4.   Widening the perspective

We have already seen that all tourism facilities involve the use and transformation of resources, natural and man-made. We are aware that these internal operations do not take place in a vacuum but also have repercussions outside the organization itself so that performance becomes both an internal and external issue. It therefore needs to be addressed from a variety of perspectives.

5.   Measuring the effects of tourism activity

Tourism activity can be assessed at various levels: the scale, type and nature of the attraction under consideration being of paramount importance. The large scale Euro Disney development near Paris will have effects at international, national, regional and local levels. By comparison, a doll's house museum at a Devon seaside resort will have an almost exclusively local impact. The type of resources used will also substantially affect the measurement criteria to be employed: man-made commercial ventures may in some circumstances be more easily assessed by financial and quantitative recorded data whereas other attractions may have significant aesthetic, ecological or conservation impacts that are virtually impossible to embody comprehensively in an objective, quantified way.

6.   The stakeholder approach

A useful starting point to integrate these diverse perspectives is to use a *stakeholder* approach in the first instance, to identify all the various parties that are affected by an organization's operations. Taking a typical tourist attraction owned by a public limited company (plc) (for example, Warwick Castle) we could identify the interested parties as:

(a) *Visitors* – who will be concerned with the nature of the experience delivered relative to their expenditure of time and money. In other words *perceived value/quality* relationships will be the criteria by which they will judge the organization and appraise its performance.
(b) *Employees* – concerned with their conditions of employment and

service, rewards payable, future prospects in terms of promotion, growth and/or stability.

(c) *Shareholders* – will be concerned with the profitability and the relative return on their capital invested through dividend payments or capital growth.

(d) *Society* – will be concerned and indeed affected in a less direct, but no less significant way by wider impacts involving economic, socio-cultural and environmental effects. On the benefit side, incomes generated, jobs created and foreign earnings will need to be offset against the negative effects of adverse aesthetic consequences, congestion problems or other detrimental environmental impacts.

7. Criteria for performance assessment

Implicit in this stakeholder approach is the recognition that criteria for performance assessment will differ in that they reflect diverse perspectives. In general, visitors and employees will have personal and often highly subjective perspectives, making relative comparisons difficult but not impossible. Shareholders will have more homogeneous quantitative criteria allowing relative comparisons for the profit-orientated sector. In ventures where joint initiatives or non-profit making considerations are involved, the stakeholders themselves may have diverse motivations or objectives. Local authorities will be concerned at community reactions and public opinion, thus invalidating conventional quantitative criteria of evaluation. Trusts may be driven by complex motives or established practices that are not rigorously appraised and so pose problems for objective quantification.

8. The pivotal role of the visitor

We have already stressed the pivotal role of the visitor in tourism facility management so in the next chapter we will start evaluating performance from their perspective.

11
Meeting customer needs

1. Customer expectations

We have already met the idea that customers come to tourism attractions with prior expectations that have been cumulatively built up through:

(a) verbal information from friends and acquaintances;
(b) media sources;
(c) advertising and promotion campaigns;
(d) previous visits; and/or
(e) visit to other attractions.

Their expectations are therefore a complex weave of highly qualitative data about a primarily intangible activity: the quality standards expected, though real, are necessarily difficult to identify. There is general recognition in the industry that customers have increasing expectations and are wishing to upgrade the service that they receive accordingly.

2. Quality

This is increasingly regarded as a major determinant of success. PIMS (Profit Impact Market Strategy) studies in the USA rank customer perceived quality as one of the four most important variables in deciding profitability. There is tacit agreement that although 'exact' measures of quality may be difficult to establish in a comparative sense, the absence of quality is immediately apparent. In other words we all know when it has not been achieved.

3. Measuring quality

At a simplistic level this can be approached by asking whether the service delivered conforms to the set *specification requirements*. Problems frequently arise from the fact that the specification of the provider is sometimes different from that of the visitor. This has been explored by separating the final output from the context in which it is delivered. Gronroos (1983) emphasized the difference between what is delivered in a *technical* sense and what he termed the *functional* aspect, which relates to the delivery process itself. In similar vein Lehtinen (1983) distinguishes between *process quality* which is judged during the service and *output quality* which is judged in retrospect, after the service is completed.

4. Quality performance indicators

In seeking the definitive answer to quality, Berry, Zeithaml and Parasuraman (1985) identified a whole series of features that can be usefully used as performance indicators. The ones with most relevance to tourism are:

(a) *reliability*
(b) *responsiveness*
(c) *competence*
(d) *access*
(e) *courtesy*
(f) *communication*
(g) *security*, and above all
(h) *understanding the customer.*

This last point fits in with the work of Wyckoff (Lovelock 1988) who divides quality into components based on designed quality standards, the conformity to these and the fitness of the design of the whole strategy for meeting customer needs.

5. Is the customer satisfied?

At a practical level, the most useful approach is to appraise the level of visitor satisfaction derived from the experience and to compare this with their expectations. Negative dissatisfaction will occur if expectations are greater than satisfaction; positive satisfaction if expectations are less than satisfaction. A uniform experience may, therefore, result in different ratings if prior expectations vary. Customers with low expectations may, after encountering a particular experience, appear highly satisfied while another customer with high initial expectations can appear highly dissatisfied, even though the actual experience and delivery system was identical. Building up false expectations is a major cause of dissatisfaction when process or output quality do not measure up. It is then important to be able to appraise delivery standards and ensure that at least the minimum intended level is always achieved.

6. Initial information

Monitoring standards needs to start prior to arrival when information instigating the visit is first received: leaflets/literature need reviewing, advertisements should be monitored and verbal information checked (for example, accuracy of recorded telephone messages and response times). En route signposting, directions for admittance, parking and so on, are the next aspects, followed by admission procedure. Time spent queuing, ticketing and being greeted at reception should be monitored, the latter being quite crucial, since it offers the first contact with staff and the customer care that is to be delivered.

7. Facilities and internal procedures

These reflect the nature of the facility. Design, layouts, interpretation, signposting, facilities and so on, as part of operations management (*see* Chapter 10), will be evaluated by visitors and can equally be appraised by staff. Cleanliness, courtesy, responsiveness and some of the other components in Berry, Zeithaml and Parasuraman's list will be relevant. Auditing these requires meticulous care.

8. Customer auditing

Customer auditing can be undertaken in a variety of ways:

(a) *Employing professionals* to visit as customers who through experiencing the service direct can assess whether actual delivery meets preset standards. This can be done on a strict entry-to-exit checklist basis or may be conducted in a fashion which allows the auditor greater discretion and flexibility to check staff attitudes, other visitors' comments and other factors.

(b) *Questionnaires* covering all aspects of the experience may be issued regularly to a sample of visitors or more intensively if specific aspects need to be checked.

(c) *Interviews* may be conducted, again on a random routine basis, or with a specific purpose in mind. There are advantages and drawbacks to this approach. Skilled, trained interviewers are needed for unbiased feedback.

Example _____

At British Airports Authority (BAA) 'continuously improving quality of service' is one of their stated objectives. In meeting this goal, feedback from written comments is supplemented by face-to-face interviews. In 1990/1 a total of 110,000 people were interviewed for the Quality of

Service Monitor (QSM), appraising aspects of airport service for arrivals and departures. Results are circulated to corporate and airport management each month and managers are required to achieve improvements when areas of weakness are exposed. Each score is a weighted average of the individual aspects covered under the relevant heading. Managers are able to measure their performances against other managers in the group.

Grouped QSM results 1990/91

	Heathrow	Gatwick	Stanstead
Value for money	3.1	3.3	3.5
Cleanliness	3.8	3.9	4.0
Mechanical assistance	3.9	3.9	3.8
Procedures	3.7	4.0	4.0
Comfort	3.8	4.0	3.9
Congestion	3.4	3.7	3.9
BAA staff	4.0	4.2	4.4

Rating scale: 5 = Excellent; 4 = Good; 3 = Average;
2 = Poor; 1 = Extremely poor.

(d) *Customer clinics* can be conducted to review expectations and delivery. Though often used to assess expectations of new attractions prior to opening as a means of ironing out teething troubles, there are substantial advantages to be obtained by using selected groups to give honest feedback on a regular basis.

(e) *Comments and suggestion boxes* are another source of performance feedback.

(f) *Monitoring complaints.* Though in theory these should not occur if quality standards are maintained consistently they can be a tremendous source of valuable information if processed correctly. Distinctions need to be drawn between the causes of complaints – in particular whether they are the result of the system, procedures or the staff. Staff should be trained to handle complaints with appropriate empathy and listening skills and also be empowered to mitigate grievances to improve customer satisfaction. Customer care training in this area is essential.

9. Monitoring competitors

Keeping an eye on the competition is an essential aspect of performance appraisal since quality ratings are, in practice, always relative. It is important to keep up with 'best practice' but preferably to be ahead of one's competitors. Allowing staff to visit competitors, equipped with pencil and paper to record the strengths and weaknesses will provide interesting feedback as well as heightening self-awareness of their own performances.

10. Quality circles

Quality circles are one of the techniques that have been used in manufacturing to improve quality control. Although doubts have been cast on their use, they have interesting implications for service staff. In essence they offer a bottom-up approach, seeking solutions to problems encountered by staff or visitors. Operating with management support (and resources) a voluntary, preferably, but sometimes selected team, led by a series of leaders in rotation, address issues of concern within the working environment and offer potential solutions. In an appropriate culture this can be very effective in providing impetus for change and increasing motivation and involvement. However, the reverse is also true and can lead to rapid disillusionment if follow-up action is not forthcoming from management.

11. Quality assurance

Investing in quality assurance will take a tourist attraction some way towards meeting customer needs. Knowing customer expectations and understanding their motivation can facilitate the design of appropriate experiences. Delivering these will involve monitoring quality and at the same time identifying gaps or problems that need to be addressed to retain the competitive edge that is the secret of success in the industry. In the leisure industry some organizations have gone a considerable way to ensuring all round quality by obtaining British Standards 5750. The Oasis at Swindon is one example of a leisure centre that, having taken the quality issue very seriously in their application for BS5750, now regard it as an extremely useful means of focusing on operation procedures to ensure all round quality when meeting the needs of the customer.

12. Reading the trend indicators

Other indicators that would reflect how well customer needs are being met might be:

(a) the number of visitors and their trend patterns compared with the rest of the industry or competitors;
(b) position in industry league tables;

(c) revenue figures and their relative trends;
(d) awards obtained for outstanding performance or contributions;
for example:

(*i*) The Green Tourism Award given to Center Parcs in 1991 for its environmental conservation and care;
(*ii*) Museum of the Year Award to York National Railway Museum in 1991 for redevelopment and interpretation;
(*iii*) England's Visitor Attraction of the Year which went to White Cliffs Experience at Dover for its outstanding performance;
(*iv*) More unusual, but no less relevant from the visitor's perspective would be the Tourism For All Award given in recognition of the facilities provided for the visually impaired at Flambards, with the help of GEC Marconi's IT expertise and financial support from the Royal National Institute for the Blind.
(*v*) The Scottish Thistle Awards cover similar categories to reward individuals and organizations in the industry who set standards for the rest to emulate.
(*vi*) At a national level there is a Come to Britain Trophy that carries a great deal of prestige and was recently given to the new Lanark visitor centre in Scotland.

These accolades indicate the high standards of excellence and the innovative nature of the experience being delivered and will be reflected in the additional appraisal criteria covered in the next chapter.

Progress test 11

For students

S1. Why should customer needs be a main focus for appraisal?

S2. What influences visitor expectations? **(1)**

S3. Identify and compare the approaches that have been developed for measuring quality. **(3, 4)**

S4. Why is the focus on expectations useful? **(5)**

S5. What is meant by customer auditing? **(8)**

S6. Visit a tourist attraction and undertake your own audit. **(6, 7)**

S7. Why might the use of quality circles be particularly relevant to tourism related enterprises? **(10 and Chapter 5)**

S8. What quantitative information could be used to reflect visitor satisfaction? **(12)**

For managers and practitioners

M1. Are customer needs regularly reviewed in your organization? If so, how? If not, what would be the advantages of doing so?

M2. What factors influence visitor expectations prior to their visit to your facility? **(1)**

M3. Which of the defined quality measurement approaches would be most useful in your organization? **(3)**

M4. Of the quality indicators listed by Berry, Zeithaml and Parasuraman (1985) which are the most applicable to your facility? **(4)**

M5. Set out an appropriate programme for customer auditing in your facility. **(8)**

M6. Explore whether quality circles have, or could be used, in your organization? **(10)**

M7. Compare your organization with a competitor and set out a league table for relative performance in meeting customer needs.

M8. Does your organization run a quality assurance programme? **(11)**

12

Appraisal criteria

1. **Applying the systems approach**
   We have already used the systems approach to examining a business as a transformation process (*see* Fig. 12.1).

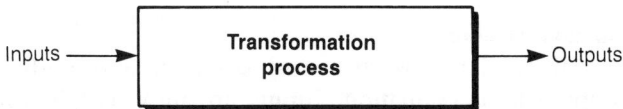

Inputs ⟶ **Transformation process** ⟶ Outputs

Figure 12.1 *The transformation process*

This is a most useful starting point for measuring performance since it relates resources used to the output produced. From this relationship we can begin to measure the effectiveness and efficiency of the organization, from both an internal perspective (owners and employees) and an external perspective (visitors, shareholders and society at large).

2. **Effectiveness**
   This is a measure of how well management has met its objectives; it may be seen as a 'mission accomplished' type of approach. The clarity and nature of the objectives set will determine the ease of measuring how far they have been achieved. For example, a tourist attraction, such as a theme park, may set as one of its objectives an increase in the number of visitors, by a percentage target figure, for a particular season. The extent to which such an objective has been met at the end of the season is relatively easy to measure. If the objective had been to raise the productivity of employees then more difficult, but not impossible, measurement problems would have been involved. As we have seen in Chapter 3, many objectives are formulated in qualitative, rather than quantitative terms, such as improving customer care and

visitor experience. Such objectives, concerned with the intangibles of the tourist industry, are more difficult to appraise and evaluate.

3.   Efficiency

This is represented by the maximization of output from the resources used and all organizations, whether in the private or the public sector, are concerned with their efficiency in these terms. There are in theory two approaches to efficiency: one involves minimizing resource inputs to obtain a specified output level and the other is to maximize the output with given inputs. It is not, however, easy to measure efficiency and it is doubtful whether a complete measure is possible at all; a selective or partial approach has inevitably to be adopted.

4.   Financial efficiency

Financial efficiency is the most common and perhaps the easiest approach to evaluation. Inputs are measured in financial terms (costs, payments made) and related to the value of output. Readers will recognize this as synonymous with profitability. Maximizing the 'value added' ensures high financial efficiency. But high profits on their own do not always signal overall efficiency; an enterprise which enjoys a monopolistic position in the market place can charge high prices and so achieve a high added value, in spite of being technically inefficient in the way it uses its resources. The hotel industry has often been criticized because of its high energy consumption which represents technical inefficiency in the way it uses natural energy resources. Heritage attractions may inflate current profits by inadequate conservation work.

5.   Social efficiency

Of increasing concern, not merely in the UK but worldwide, is social efficiency, since it is recognized that *all* business activity has repercussions on society and the environment. Tourism gives rise to negative impacts and spillover effects, arising from congestion, noise and other ecological or pollution effects. It may influence and infringe adversely on the cultural and social habits of the local host population. None of these effects is recorded in the financial records of an organization but need to be offset against the positive benefits that tourism activity can offer society as a whole. Measuring this aggregate impact effect is difficult if stakeholders have different perspectives on the benefits and costs. To some extent the problems are correlated to the size, ownership and nature of the attraction. Size is self-explanatory because impacts will be immediately observable; ownership poses more complex issues since non-profit-making bodies are seen as custodians of societies' interests for current and future generations. The resources used become of significant concern in the context of sustainable and renewable resources. A specific approach is usually required rather than a generalized one. Environmental impact assessments are now required in the UK when planning permission for any significant tourism development is sought. As a public relations exercise this information will be supplemented by employment offered, incomes generated, investment undertaken, foreign exchange earnings, preservation and conservation expenditures and so on, if applicable.

6. Profitability, growth and stability
The major objectives built into the strategic plans of private sector organizations are profitability, growth and stability. They will, therefore, loom large in the internal appraisal process. The following criteria will be used as targets or indicators for assessment:

(a) profitability on capital employed (*see* Chapter 9)
(b) productivity, particularly labour
(c) margins on sales
(d) cost and revenue patterns
(e) value added
(f) market share
(g) visitor expenditure per head
(h) visitor numbers and repeat visits
(i) share prices and trends.

7. Qualitative objectives in the appraisal process
Public sector or non-profit making organizations may well have more qualitative objectives that will be reflected in their appraisal process. These may include educational roles, services to disadvantaged groups in society, or image enhancement through prestige developments that bring status or environmental improvements. Over the last 10 years a more commercial outlook has developed within the public sector and a greater emphasis is given to quantifiable indicators including cost effectiveness. Under competitive contract tendering this process has been formalized so that financial criteria are now very significant.

8.   **The link between appraisal and budgeting control**
Internal appraisal criteria link the outcome of organizations to their budgeting and control processes (*see* Chapter 9). In this context the measurement of the relationships between the actual inputs and outputs of any organization can be compared with budgeted and planned. If the difference between these give cause for concern then new standards and new approaches to the transformation process will need to be worked out so that the overall efficiency and effectiveness of the organization can be improved. In this context inter-firm comparisons are often used in many industries other than tourism to provide comparative reference points. The hotel industry has gone some way in this direction and the Association of Independent Museums is beginning to share useful data. A great deal of cooperation and survey work is needed for a thorough cross-sector analysis in the tourist industry but partial comparisons can be undertaken by focusing on data that is published and readily accessible (for example, Dun and Bradstreet and Jordans reports derived from company accounts)

9.   In conclusion, effective performance appraisal should provide the answers to the following questions:

(a) How effective is the transformation process?
(b) To what extent is it efficient?
(c) What are the benefits that accrue and to whom?
(d) What costs are involved and who bears them?
(e) Do the benefits outweigh the costs for current and future generations?

Progress test 12

For students

S1. Define effectiveness. (**2**)

S2. Define efficiency. (**3**)

S3. Why is efficiency much more difficult to measure than effectiveness? (**4, 5**)

S4. Why might profits not be synonymous with efficient resource use? Give examples from the tourism industry. (**3, 4, 5**)

S5. Examine the annual reports of three private sector organizations in the tourism industry. Abstract the information relating to performance. Is it sufficiently comprehensive to provide an overall performance picture? **(6)**

S6. Examine the annual reports of a non-profit making organization in the tourism industry. How does the information differ from private sector reports. **(7)**

S7. What performance indicators would be most useful for internal control purposes? **(8)**

S8. What timescales should be adopted when appraising tourism attractions? Would you treat Stonehenge, Westminster Abbey, Alton Towers and your local leisure complex in the same way? **(9)**

Managers and practitioners

M1. How is the effectiveness of your organization measured? **(2)**

M2. Is the efficiency of your organization measured? **(3)**

M3. Is your organization either profitable and efficient or efficient and not profitable? **(3, 4, 5)**

M4. Obtain a copy of your organization's annual report. To what extent does the information published in it allow outsiders to appraise its overall performance? What further information should in your opinion be included? **(6, 7)**

M5. If you work for a profit (non-profit) orientated organization obtain a non-profit (profit) orientated organization's report and examine the differences in approach and information Explain what you observe. **(6, 7)**

M6. What indicators are used inside your organization for measuring performance and control purposes? **(6, 7)**

Part six

Interfacing with the environment

Introduction to part six

We have frequently referred to the fact that every organization
operates within an environmental setting that simultaneously
imposes constraints and offers opportunities. In this section we set
out to review explicitly the most crucial aspects and issues that
should be addressed by managers in their decision making when
interfacing with the complex and dynamic environment of the
tourism industry.

13

Managing change and fostering enterprise

1. The need to monitor change

Figure 13.1 summarizes the setting in which organizations operate: the diversity of the environmental influences are apparent and we have already covered some of the influences in detail.

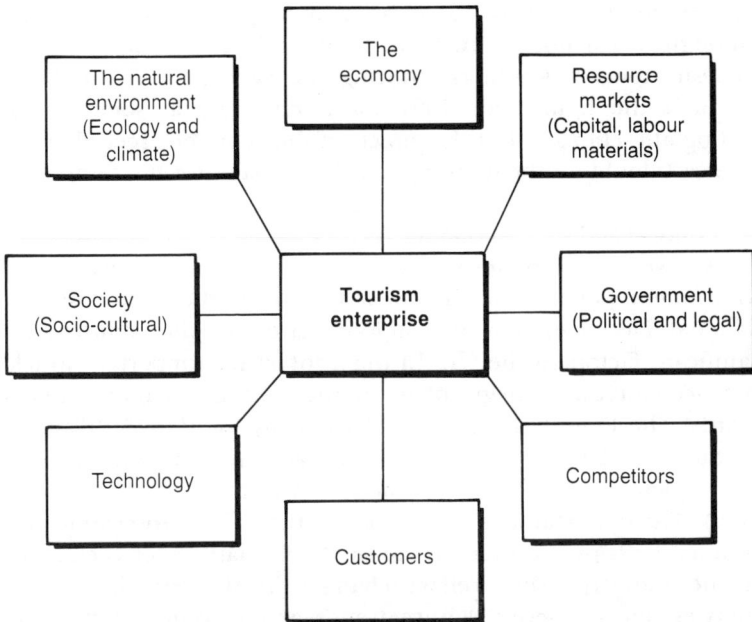

Figure 13.1 *Environmental influences*

Successful organizations are able to identify the key external variables relevant to their performance and focus their energies in these areas so that change can be monitored, assessed and action taken at an appropriate level.

2. Interpreting the external environment.

The main environmental influences impinging on the decision making process in tourism enterprises can be classified as economic, socio-cultural, political, technological and/or natural ecological and climatic. Their actual impact will vary through time and according to the activity, size, corporate form and objectives of the individual enterprise. The levels at which these influences will need to be appraised may range from local or regional to national or global. The important point, from a strategic stance, is to assess the *key* features and monitor these with great care and precision.

3. The anticipated growth of tourism

At a global level it is anticipated that the level of tourism activity will continue to rise at approx 4–5.5 per cent per annum throughout the 1990s. Growth is anticipated within Europe, although it will not be uniform. In the UK, it was expected that domestic tourism would rise during the early part of the 1990s, although the figures for 1991 for attendances at some of the leading attractions reflect the effects of the economic recession and have cast doubt on the more optimistic estimates for the future.

4. Political and socio-economic factors

As well as monitoring overall activity levels, changes in government policy (now channelled through the Department of National Heritage) and the support given to the industry, are significant factors in the UK. In this context it is important to take into account the strategic plans of the BTA and national tourist boards. The English Tourist Board's strategy for 1991–5: 'Planning for Success' (ETB 1990) builds on the achievements that followed the implementation of the earlier 'A Vision for England' (ETB 1988). The opportunities are set out on the basis of forecast growth in domestic trips and overseas visitors to give targets for each sector of the industry. They reflect changes in demographic trends, lifestyles, income levels, leisure trends and consumer tastes. The area most relevant to tourism enterprises (day trips) is estimated to run at 550 million annually, generating nearly £5 billion, an increase of 12–15 per cent by 1995.

5. Planning for success (ETB)

The plan sets out four major challenges:

(a) mounting international competition especially from Europe;

(b) pressure to balance the needs of tourism with the need to preserve the environment;
(c) an urgent need to improve transport and communication;
(d) recruiting, training and motivating a skilled workforce in a competitive labour market.

Detailed changes suggested as necessary include:

(*i*) maintaining balance and harmony with the environment as set out in Chapter 14;
(*ii*) improvement of value for money and quality through upgrading and improved visitor management;
(*iii*) improvements in quality of training and recruitment leading to improved professionalism;
(*vi*) improved innovative marketing.

At a regional and local level the plans of regional tourist boards and local authorities would also need to be taken into account when writing the overall scenario and assessing the relevant variables. The ETB is running a seaside resorts campaign in 1992 and an Industrial Heritage Year in 1993. The Welsh and Scottish tourist boards have separate strategy plans.

6. Anticipating change

Recognizing the need for change is an important responsibility and function of management since planned change is positive and can be undertaken with minimum stress. Many organizations are forced into change only when their survival is seen to be under threat. Although there may be some occasions when unexpected and non-predictable changes occur, such as wars or freak climatic conditions, most changes in the external environment are incremental and can be anticipated at least in a directional sense if not with total accuracy.

7. Recognizing types of change

A distinction should be drawn between imposed change and desired change. Imposed change comes from a recognition that change *has* to occur that is, it is coerced. It may be the result of social, economic, technological, regulatory influences or even competitors' performance and it is usually external factors which are the coercive force. Desired change may be internally driven and reflect the recognition that 'there are better ways of doing old things' so that effectiveness or efficiency can be improved. Even voluntary change of this nature is usually difficult to implement since there is an inbuilt inertia in most individuals and organizations and a resistance to change.

8. Overcoming resistance to change

Resistance to change is much more widespread than individuals care to admit. It is linked to the security derived from the familiar. The unknown poses challenges with which many people find it difficult to cope: the uncertainty is unsettling and the ambiguity disturbing. Change requires the termination of practices that have become routine and systematic, attitudes have to be realigned and often new skills have to be learned or developed.

9. Developing management policies

In a scenario where adaptability and flexibility are the requirements for success, management should realize the high priority that will need to be given to policies that eliminate resistance to change. These may well include:

(a) participative management style;
(b) building of trust through open and frequent communication between all levels of staff and management;
(c) flexible work teams with a common purpose/culture;
(d) appropriate training in required skills and knowledge.

In a business where strategic change has already been introduced it can be much easier to introduce plans and implement dramatic adjustments, if necessary in the event of unforeseen crises.

10. Implementing change

Implementing change is as we have seen best carried out in an atmosphere of trust but will also require that all staff who are affected know *why, what, how,* and *when* changes are to be made. In other words they will need to be briefed on:

(a) the objectives, rationale and expected outcomes;
(b) the extent and nature of the changes;
(c) the procedures and methods to be employed;
(d) the timescales involved.

11. Managing change

All the stages are important but establishing the reason is the main hurdle. Once staff have accepted that change is desirable they will be willing to own the management of the process itself. Incremental and gradual changes in order to build up confidence are ideal if time permits, or if substantial cultural blocks are acting as barriers. Well organized, smooth changes establish trust and minimize stress. Sometimes, however, sharp shock treatment may be the only option, especially if there is a marked and persistent reluctance to change attitudes and the previous strategies have been tried.

12. Innovation and creativity
These are essential characteristics of a progressive tourism enterprise. They ensure that new ideas, new products, new processes and new ways of managing are introduced.

(a) *Product innovation* is probably the most easily identifiable form of innovation and numerous examples can be used as illustrations. These include products within existing attractions, for example, novel theme park rides or computer-enhanced interpretation in museums. Completely new products have been developed. Industrial tourism has been innovative and extremely successful in many areas of the UK. The rapid rise to fame of Cadbury World is perhaps much less surprising than the unexpected success of the Sellafield nuclear reprocessing plant in Cumbria in attracting visitors. Bringing creative ideas to fruition is very significant for new industries where technical possibilities and market needs offer opportunities for links in original ways.

(b) *Process innovation* though very significant from an operations perspective is not so easily observed: the use of desk-top publishing for promotional material or timed ticketing to control visitor flows in special events illustrate the increasingly sophisticated uses of information technology (IT) within enterprises. Introducing new ways of managing enterprises also demands creativity. Organizational design is an area where this may be observed as the task is to match capabilities with demands in terms of resource use. Habit, inertia and bureaucracy in this context can be defeated by originality and creativity although balancing the need for creativity against the need for structure and control is as we have seen in Chapter 4 an immensely difficult task.

13. Entrepreneurship
Kao (1989) has observed entrepreneurship to be 'the human and organizational process by which innovation takes place' and

there are obviously strong links between creativity and entrepreneurship. They are not however identical since new ideas can be thought of without implementing them in practice. It is this ability to get things done that distinguishes the true entrepreneur who sees or searches for opportunities to exploit and who is willing to take on the risks involved.

14. Entrepreneurs in action

The tourism industry has produced a large number of well known entrepreneurial figures. During the 1980s Peter De Savery undertook substantial developments at John O'Groats, Littlecote, and Land's End. A self-professed 'creator and developer' and 'land enhancement specialist' but 'not a caretaker' he has now sold many of his developments to other companies. Richard Branson, the creator of Virgin Airways, now has plans for privatizing rail routes. He has been able to identify commercial opportunities and, via skilful publicity and marketing, exploit them in a uniquely entrepreneurial fashion. In the 1992 Tourism UK awards Virgin was awarded top prize for their off-peak travel promotions between the US and the UK. Not all entrepreneurs remain successful. John Broome's success at Alton Towers underpinned his initial moves to develop Battersea as a major tourism attraction, but a series of problems ended in the sale of Alton Towers to Pearsons plc and Battersea remains undeveloped.

On a smaller scale the industry has many examples of individuals who have diversified into the industry. Sheep World in Devon is an example of a farmer's diversification policy: the Rare Breeds Park in the Cotswolds developed out of the founder's hobby and interest in the genetic conservation of domestic farm animals. Many small museums, gardens and water mills and so on, have a similar history.

15. Intrapreneurial organizations

Large scale organizations can also be intrapreneurial, in the sense that they are innovative and risk taking. Center Parcs provides an example of a large organization that correctly predicted holiday and environmental trends and exploited them to advantage; Heritage Projects (UK) perceived how heritage combined with modern technology could consistently attract large numbers of visitors at Jorvik and the concept has been extended to other centres. Local authorities have developed themed museum complexes and clustered heritage sites to advantage, in locations such as Portsmouth, Gloucester and Liverpool.

16. Change for the future
    The rapid growth and development of tourism enterprises in an era of limited overall economic growth is proof that the industry is enterprising and innovative. The future requires that creative thinking, which defeats habit by originality, must continue to play a major role in the industry to provide on-going success and a challenge for managers.

Progress test 13

For students

S1. What are the key factors in the environment that need to be monitored by tourism enterprises (a) operating locally, and (b) operating nationally? **(2)**

S2. Examine the most recent strategic plans produced by your national tourist board and analyze the impact they might have on tourism attractions in your area. **(2)**

S3. Why is it imperative that business organizations are able to cope with change? **(3)**

S4. How could change programmes be effectively implemented in an organization? Would the size of the organization influence the strategy? **(4, 5)**

S5. Find examples of innovations and creativity from tourist attractions with which you are familiar. Try and find out who initiated them. **(6)**

S6. How would you define entrepreneurship? Illustrate your definition with examples of behaviour from the tourism industry. **(7)**

S7. What is meant by an intrapreneurial organization? Illustrate with examples from the tourism industry. **(8)**

S8. Choose a tourism organization that has been established for at least five years. Review its development and pinpoint how it has responded to the changing external environment in which it operates.

For managers and practitioners

M1. What are the key factors in the environment that should be monitored by your organization? **(1)**

M2. To what extent are the strategic plans developed by your national and/or your regional tourist boards taken into account when your organization undertakes its planning? **(2)**

M3. Would you classify your organization as flexible and adaptable? If yes, give examples to illustrate. If no, why not?

M4. Have there been any deliberate change policies introduced in your organization ? Reflect on the reason(s) for their introduction and attempt to appraise the outcome. **(4, 5)**

M5. If you work in a small organization does the owner fit the entrepreneurial definition? Justify your answer. **(7)**

M6. If you work for a large organization is it intrapreneurial? Justify your answer. **(8)**

M7. Choose a tourism organization which has been in existence for at least five years (your own or maybe a competitor). Review its development and appraise the extent to which it has adapted to its external environment.

14

Tourism enterprises and society

1. The impact of tourism on the environment

A tourism enterprise cannot exist without having an effect on the environment in which it operates: some effects will be beneficial, others will be negative. Though the debate regarding tourism impacts is not new, currently both in the UK and globally, society is increasingly sensitive to the whole question of tourism impacts. The reason for this preoccupation reflects increased public concern about the future of our environment in general and the recognition that a strategy is necessary if our 'common inheritance' is to be preserved for future generations.

2. The Tourism and Environment Task Force

Tourism is, to many, a rogue industry using the assets of the environment as a resource and, if unchecked, will erode the very base that attracted tourists in the first place. It was this concern, highlighted in the Government White Paper of 1990, that led to the setting up of the Tourism and Environment Task Force in August 1990 to review tourism and its relationship with the environment. Its conclusions and recommendations on visitor management are of direct relevance to enterprises and attractions operating in the industry.

3. The positive side of tourism

Stressing the relationships between visitors, the place and host communities the task force highlighted the positive and negative aspects that tourism can bring.

Tourism can offer opportunities including:

- bringing satisfaction and enrichment to visitors, strengthening a respect for our natural and built heritage and promoting an understanding and appreciation of other communities and cultures;

- supporting the maintenance and improvement of our heritage and ensuring its preservation for future generations;
- acting as a catalyst for the regeneration of derelict land and disused buildings;
- generating jobs and wealth, diversifying fragile economies, widening economic opportunities and stimulating investment;
- improving the quality of community life by widening choice, supporting local services and bringing social contact. (ETB 1991)

4. **The negative side of tourism**

The negative aspects of tourism can include:

(a) permanent damage to landscapes and sites;
(b) the overwhelming of local cultures;
(c) congestion through traffic and crowds;
(d) pollution through litter and noise;
(e) high maintenance and infrastructure costs.

A balance has to be struck between tourism and the environment, to avoid negative impacts and to ensure that benefits can be maintained and sustained in the long run.

The following case study was produced for the Tourism and the Environment Task Force set up by the Secretary of State in conjunction with the ETB and Department of Employment in 1990. It is intended to illustrate some of the best practice techniques and mechanisms that can be employed for effective visitor management in areas where conservation and environmental pressures exist.

Example : Dove Cottage: case study _____

Dove Cottage was Wordsworth's home from 1799–1808 and was purchased in 1890 by the Wordsworth Trust, a registered charity. In 1990 it received 87,000 visitors and its potential carrying capacity was estimated at 100,000. It is on a severely restricted access site adjacent to woodland and provides a bookshop, museum, library and restaurant.

The aim of the Trust is to display the cottage and illustrate the poet's life and work and to ensure that it remains 'the eternal possession of all who love English poetry all over the world'. It is run by a board of trustees who take professional management experience advice from Cumbria Tourist Board, Lake District National Park and the Department of Transport.

The property has to limit and control visitor numbers at certain times, yet needs to attract as many visitors as feasible in order to maintain the financial support required. To this end careful marketing is undertaken to attract selected groups, especially during off-season periods. Visitor interpretation and information is of an exceptional high standard. Strong emphasis is put on visitor care, staff training and motivation; there is a commitment to regular repair and conservation and visitor needs are constantly monitored.

Various awards reflect the standards achieved and include:

BTA Come to Britain Award 1981;
Museum of the Year Special Award 1982;
Lady Inglewood Award for Best Museum in Cumbria 1987;
Sandford Heritage Education Award 1990.

The case reflects the aspirations of non-profit making organizations that work cooperatively with other organizations in the area to achieve a balance between the needs of tourism and the conservation of the environment.

5. Environmental Impact Assessment (EIA)

This is increasingly being required both in the UK and internationally when tourism development is being considered, to highlight the positive and negative aspects. This:

(a) reviews the context in which the development is being proposed: the nature, scale, form, timing and so on;
(b) forecasts the benefits, costs and externalities and identifies by whom they will be enjoyed or shouldered;
(c) appraises alternative scenarios; and
(d) sets out the opportunities for impact alleviation and/or compensations that will be undertaken if the project is given approval.

6. Sustainability

This concept is taken from the Brundtland report on 'our common future' that defined sustainable development as 'meeting the needs of the present without compromising the ability of future generations to meet their own needs' (Brundtland Report 1987). This reflects the idea that the Earth has not been inherited from our parents but borrowed from our children and so we are custodians or trustees for future generations. We must be aware of the inherent danger that tourism can destroy itself and that tourism and the environment are mutually interdependent. Searching for harmony in this context the Task Force recommended principles that should be adopted by the industry and endorsed by the government. In particular they highlighted that:

(a) tourism operators should examine the impact of their operations on the environment and assess the extent to which these principles are met;

(b) all public and private sector organizations with responsibilities in these areas should adopt the principles and encourage their implementation.

7. Establishing sustainable principles

Principles for the development and management of sustainable tourism:

(a) The environment has an intrinsic value which outweighs its value as a tourism asset. Its enjoyment by future generations and its long-term survival must not be prejudiced by short-term considerations.

(b) Tourism should be recognized as a positive activity with the potential to benefit the community and the place as well as the visitor.

(c) The relationship between tourism and the environment must be managed so that the environment is sustainable in the long term. Tourism must not be allowed to damage the resource, prejudice its future enjoyment or bring unacceptable impacts.

(d) Tourism activities and developments should respect the scale, nature and character of the place in which they are sited

(e) In any location, harmony must be sought between the needs of the visitor, the place and the host community.

(f) In a dynamic world some change is inevitable and change can often be beneficial. Adaptation to change, however, should not be at the expense of any of these principles.

(g) The tourism industry, local authorities and environmental agencies all have a duty to respect the above principles and to work together to achieve their practical realization. (ETB 1991)

Example: Warwick Castle: case study _____

This is an annotated version of one of the cases used in the Task Force report to illustrate visitor management techniques and approaches.

The site: Warwick Castle was built between 1340 and 1395 and has been described as one of the finest medieval castles in England.

Visitors have access to: the state rooms; private apartments; ramparts; gatehouse; armoury/dungeon area; watergate tower. Additional attractions include gardens, nature walks, shops and restaurants.

The castle is a public company and is owned by the Tussauds Group, itself part of Pearson plc. Day-to-day management is by a general manager and the curator. Original objectives were to develop the castle as a tourism attraction in order to be able to maintain it. Tussauds' objectives for Warwick are to

develop the tourism business in order to achieve a commercially acceptable profit and return on investment and at the same time developing and improving the site and maintaining and preserving the building, its collections and grounds to the highest standards by a rolling programme of repair, restoration and maintenance.

Problems: there are some traffic/parking problems at busy times necessitating road signing measures to alternative parks. Queuing and bottlenecks arise on public holidays. Large visitor numbers (682,621 in 1991) cause wear and tear and visitor management is necessary.

Solutions: Visitors are controlled and kept away from sensitive areas by such measures as well defined walking areas, protection devices, daily cleaning, constant monitoring, alert and committed guides as well as regular repair and conservation. Stewards are used to look after queues, groups are guided where possible, emphasis is placed on knowledgeable, friendly and helpful staff, supplementary information is kept at hand including the use of education packs.

A carrying capacity of 750,000 is regarded as feasible but will require the dispersion of visitors into off-peak times and marketing efforts are being directed in this direction. On-going, independent quantitative market research is regularly undertaken and qualitative research when required for strategic planning.

In summary, the case illustrates how operations and marketing have to be integrated to deliver a quality experience for the visitor and also to achieve the success and status that managers seek in this industry.

---

8. Safeguarding the future

Managers in this industry carry onerous responsibilities for the future. There is an overwhelming duty to act in a socially responsible way and not to sacrifice long-run balance for short-term expediency or profits. The environmental aspects have been covered at length but there are also other obligations that fall on the shoulders of managers that we examined in Chapters 11 and 12. To reiterate, they cover responsibilities to employees, consumers and other stakeholders in current and future generations.

9. Meeting the challenge

In addition all managers will face the inherent challenges reviewed in Chapter 1 that stem from the nature of the industry. Wherever you currently work or aspire to work in the future we hope that this text will have taken you some way towards being able to meet the exciting challenges of the industry in a more effective manner.

Progress test 14

For students, managers and practitioners

1. 'Tourism erodes the base of its success.' Comment on this statement and use examples to illustrate your argument. **(2, 3, 4)**

2. Why did the Government set up the Tourism and Environment Task Force? **(2)**

3. Take a tourism development that you are familiar with and set out the benefits and costs that are associated with it. Where does the balance lie? **(3, 4)**

4. What is meant by 'sustainability'? **(6)**

5. Take the principles laid down for sustainable tourism and apply them to a proposed development in your area. **(7)**

6. Set out the arguments for making Environmental Impact Assessment compulsory for all tourism development regardless of scale. **(5)**

7. Tourism can bring with it negative and positive impacts. Set out what you think should be a code of conduct to which all managers in the industry should adhere. **(Chapters 1–14)**

Appendix 1

The case study approach to learning

These cases are included to offer an opportunity to take an integrative look at management in the tourism industry. However case studies appear to differ in content, style and length, they should be approached in the same way. A number of steps can be identified to make the best use of the material offered in the case. These are:

(a) Reading thoroughly and comprehending the case.
(b) Analyzing the information, both explicit and implicit in it.
(c) Defining the problems.
(d) Reading and understanding the questions.
(e) Using the information presented to answer the questions.
(f) Checking that the best use has been made of the information presented both directly and indirectly.

It is unlikely that any case study presented to you will have *all* the information that you feel you need to answer the questions; in real life business situations you seldom have all the information you would ideally like to solve problems. As you read it note any contradictions and areas of ambiguity.

A case study, if properly used, offers an opportunity to develop skills and competencies relevant to both students and managers. These include:

(a) Analytical skills.
(b) Creative problem solving skills.
(c) Decision making skills.
(d) Communicating skills – possibly oral as well as written.
(e) Team working skills if the case is tackled by a group.
(f) working to time constraints if a time limit is set.

For students, managers and practitioners

In the following three case studies, assume you are acting as a consultant to each of the facilities in turn and carry out the following tasks:

1. Write an appropriate mission statement for the facility which should reflect its objectives.

2. Recommend a management structure for the facility. Outline this in chart form, explaining the relationships and why this structure is appropriate.

3. Write a job description for any one of the senior management jobs shown on your chart, indicating clearly the responsibilities attached to the job and the roles its holder would have to undertake. Specify the knowledge, competences and abilities you would look for in applicants for the job.

4. Identify and rank in terms of their significance to the success of the facility the problems facing the operations manager.

5. Set out a staff reward system that could be installed both to satisfy and motivate staff at the facility.

6. Define the management aspects which the marketing manager should take into account when designing the marketing plan for the facility.

7. Recommend the ways in which the facility could use information technology to ensure that there is effective management.

8. Set out what management accounting systems should be installed at the facility.

9. How would a customer care programme contribute to the presentation of a total quality service at the facility?

10. What are likely to be the major staffing problems faced at the facility and how should they be overcome?

11. Examine the ways in which the performance of the facility could be appraised.

12. What environmental issues should be taken into account when determining strategy?

Case studies

1. The Devon Experience

The Devon Experience is a new and purpose-built holiday complex covering a large area of land in South Devon, situated to give easy access to both Dartmoor and the sea. The complex is easily accessible by road and rail. It is owned and operated by a newly formed company, the Devon Experience, which is in turn owned by a parent company, SupaLeisure. The parent company allows its subsidiaries a considerable degree of autonomy in running the facility but maintains a tight central financial control.

The Devon Experience offers accommodation at several levels and within different price ranges, from a luxury hotel to self-catering chalets, a caravan park and a camp site. Careful landscaping and design with low-level buildings set among trees are intended to give holiday-makers a feeling of spaciousness. There is a sports centre with a gymnasium and facilities for tennis, badminton and squash. There are two large weather-protected swimming pools and there are arrangements for holiday-makers to enjoy a variety of outdoor sports including sailing, windsurfing and pony-treking. There are four restaurants on the site, apart from those in the hotel, and a number of shops including a good quality supermarket. An entertainments centre will offer live entertainment, films and discos.

The Devon Experience is open all year and hopes to attract short break visitors as well as holiday-makers for longer periods. The intention is to provide a quality experience and staying there veers towards the more expensive rather than the cheaper end of the market.

2. Peverell Park

Peverell Park is a very attractive large house, parts of which date back to the 15th century, set in extensive grounds of some 500 acres in Warwickshire. It has been owned since Tudor times by members of the Peverell family, Roman Catholics who, during the Civil War of the seventeenth century, were ardent Royalists. Indeed, the house is reputed to have given shelter to Charles I after he failed to defeat the Roundheads in 1642 at the nearby battle of Edgehill.

More recently, members of the family have been engaged in banking and diplomacy in the Far East and there are extensive collections of pictures and artefacts from China and Japan in the house. After the death of the last direct descendant of the family in

1986, the house, its contents and the estate went to the National Trust.

The house already has the following facilities, since for some years the Peverall family opened it to the public:

(a) Tours of the house with heritage talks on its Civil War connections including the family chapel and the priest's hole. The oriental collections are displayed in a separate and major exhibition.

(b) Cafe and restaurant facilities.

(c) A shop selling high class souvenirs, including specially made reproductions of artefacts of the house. The Trust intends to add its usual range of products to those available in this retail outlet.

(d) A garden centre/shop specializing in herbs and original varieties of plants.

Because the grounds lend themselves to performances the Trust proposes to stage a number of events in the summer, including a week of opera and a number of special musical evenings with firework displays. There are also a number of cottages on the estate which are to be restored for holiday letting.

3.   A county museum

There are five museums in the county as a whole, of which this is one, specializing in the presentation of the county town's industrial heritage of textiles and vehicle manufacturing. These industries have now closed down. Because the town was for many years a major port the museum also houses a fine collection of trading memorabilia and artefacts from former colonial territories in Africa and Asia. For the last ten years the museum and its displays have remained virtually unchanged and its visitor numbers static. It lacks any refreshment facilities and its retailing consists of one small stall in the entrance. Its displays make no concessions to the many foreign visitors who come to the town.

The museum has recently been reorganized and now has a site manager responsible for day-to-day management, staff premises and security and a museums officer who is responsible for the displays in the museum, for special events, for its educational work and for publicity and promotion work. They are both responsible to the county council's leisure and arts department which provides technical and management support services for all the county's museums as well as direct funding through the annual budgeting process.

The museum employs some twenty people in all, mainly as wardens for security; any guiding they offer is limited and they have not been trained in any way. The museum has been told that it must increase its own revenue resources as its funding from the county council will be progressively reduced. The museum is to introduce an admission charge.

Bibliography and further reading

Adair, J. (1983), *Effective leadership*, Gower.

Aldefer, C.P. (1972), *Existence, relatedness and growth*, Collier Macmillan.

Belbin, R.M. (1981), *Management teams – Why they succeed or fail*, Heinemann.

Bentley, J.L. (1989), *Center Parcs*, Pavic Publications.

Berry, L.L., Zeithaml,V.A. and Parasuraman, A. (1985), 'Quality counts in services too', *Business horizons*, May-June.

Blake, R. and Mouton, J. (1964), *The managerial grid*, Gulf Publishing Co., Houston, Texas.

Booms, B.H. and Bitner, M.J. (1981), 'Marketing strategies and organisation structures for service firms' in *Marketing of services*, American Marketing Association.

British Tourist Authority (BTA) (1988), *Strategy for growth 1989–93*.

British Tourist Board (BTB) (1988), *Visitor attraction survey*, annual, BTB.

Brundtland Report (1987), *Our common future*, World Commission on Environment and Development.

Child, J. (1988), *Organization*, 2nd edition, Paul Chapman Publishing.

Cooper, C. (ed.) (1991), *Progress in tourism, recreation and hospitality research*, Frances Pinter.

Drucker, P.F. (1979), *Management*, Pan.

Employment Gazette, monthly publication containing statistics and special surveys of the industry, HMSO.

English Tourist Board (ETB) (1988), *A vision for England*.
 (1990), *Planning for success 1991–95*.
 (1991), *Tourism and the environment – maintaining the balance*.

Fayol, H. (1949), *General and industrial management*, Pitman Publishing.

Ferguson, D.H. and Berger, F. (1984), *Restaurant Managers: What do they really do?*, Cornell, HRA Quarterly, p. 30.

Gronroos, C. (1983), *Strategic management and marketing in the service sector*, MSI Cambridge.

Handy, C.B. (1985), *Understanding organizations*, Penguin.

Harris, N.D. (1989), *Service operations management*, Cassell.

Herzberg, F. (1966), *Work and the nature of man*, World Publishing Co., New York, USA.

Hicks, H.C. and Gillett, C.R. (1985), *Management*, McGraw Hill.

Holloway, J.C. and Plant, R.V. (1992), *Marketing for tourism*, 2nd edition, Pitman Publishing.

Hunt, J.W. (1986), *Managing people at work*, 2nd edition, McGraw-Hill.

Johnson, P. and Thomas, B. (1992), *Tourism, museums and the local economy*, Edward Elgar.

Jones, P. (ed.) (1989), *Management in service industries*, Pitman Publishing.

Kakabadse, A., Ludlow, R. and Vinnicombe, S. (1988), *Working in organisations*, Penguin.

Kao, J. (1989), *Entrepreneurship, creativity and organisation*, Prentice Hall.

Kotler, P. (1989), *Marketing management*, Prentice Hall.
  (1990), *Principles of marketing*, Prentice Hall.

Kotter, J.P. (1982), 'What effective general managers really do', *Harvard Business Review*, vol. 60, no. 6.

Krippendorf, J. (1987), *The holiday-makers – understanding the impact of leisure and travel*, Heinemann.

Lehtinen, J.R. (1983), 'Customer-orientated service system', *Service management institute working paper*, Finland.

Lovelock, C.H. (ed.) (1988), *Managing Services*, Prentice Hall.

McClelland, D.C. (1976), *The achieving society*, Irvington.

McGregor, D. (1964), *The human side of enterprise*, McGraw-Hill.

Maslow, A.H. (1987), *Motivation and personality*, 3rd edition, Harper and Row.

Mayo, G.E. (1933), *The human problems of an industrial civilisation*, Macmillan, New York.

Middleton, V.T.C. (1988), *Marketing in travel and tourism*, Heinemann.

Minkes, A.L. (1987), *The entrepreneurial manager*, Penguin.

Mintzberg, H. (1973), *The nature of managerial work*, Harper and Row, New York.

Moores, B. (1986), *Are they being served?*, Philip Allen.

Mullins, L. (1989), *Management and organisational behaviour*, 2nd edition, Pitman Publishing.

Murdick, R.G., Render, B. and Russell, R.S. (1990), *Service operations management*, Allyn and Bacon.

Murphy, P.E. (1985), *Tourism: a community approach*, Methuen.

National Economic Development Council (NEDC) (1991), *Developing managers for tourism*.
    (1992), *UK Tourism – competing for growth*, NEDO.

Normann, R. (1991), *Service management: Strategy and leadership in Service Business*, John Wiley.

Oxford Centre for Tourism and Leisure Studies (OCTALS) (1992), *Oxford Visitor Study*.

Peters, T.J. and Waterman, R.H. (1982), *In search of excellence*, Harper and Row, New York.

Peters, T.J. and Austin, N. (1986), *A passion for excellence*, Fontana.

Porter, L.W. and Lawler, E.E. (1968), *Managerial attitudes and performance*, Irwin.

Porter, M.E. (1985), *Competitive advantage – creating and sustaining superior performance*, Free Press.

Quinn, R.E., Faerman, S.R., Thompson, M.P., McGrath, M.R. (1990), *Becoming a master manager*, Wiley.

Sasser, W.E. (1978), *Management of service operations*, Allyn and Bacon.

Stewart, R. (1976), *Contrasts in management*, McGraw-Hill.

Thompson, J.L. (1990), *Strategic management*, Chapman and Hall.

Tuckman, B.W. (1965), 'Development sequence in small groups', *Psychological Bulletin*, vol. 63.

Voss, C. (ed.) (1985), *Operations management in service industries and the public sector*, Wiley, New York.

Vroom, V.H. (1964), *Work and motivation*, Wiley, New York.

Ward, J. (1991), *Tourism in Action*, Stanley Thornes (Publishers) Ltd.

Wilson, D.C. and Rosenfeld, R.H. (1990), *Managing organisations*, McGraw-Hill.

Wild, R. (1984), *Productions and operations management*, 3rd edition, Holt, Rinehart and Winston.

Witt, S.F. and Mountinho, L. (1989), *Tourism marketing and management handbook*, Prentice Hall.

Index

planning function 23, 26–7, 35–6, 107, 109, 125
Porter, M.E. 38, 39, 76
portfolio analysis 38–9, 75, 106
preference shares 104
pricing 74, 76, 78, 80–82, 86, 112
private limited company 14
product life-cycle 75
profitability 33, 35, 36, 38, 47, 107, 111, 112, 134, 136, 144, 145
project management 125
promotion 65, 78, 82, 83, 86, 117, 121, 134, 136
public limited company 14
public relations 83
purchasing 16, 116, 123, 124, 128

quality
  circles 140
  control 116, 124
  measurement 136–140
  service/product 17–18, 78, 83, 84, 123
  staff 91, 93, 95
quangos 16
Queen's Moat 98
queuing 12, 122, 123, 138, 163
Quinn, R.E. 27–8

Rare Breeds Park 156
recruitment 17, 22, 56, 83, 91, 92, 153
resource allocation 109

scheduling 12, 28, 74, 116, 121, 122, 125
selection 15, 29, 56, 78, 82, 84, 91, 92, 95, 117, 118
St Paul's Cathedral 6
Sellafield 155
Science Museum 85
shareholders 14, 15, 21, 33, 101–104, 110, 111, 134, 143
Sheep World 156
sites 7, 82, 117, 157, 160
situation analysis 36
social responsibility 18
sole proprietors 12–14
specialisation 45
Sports Council 17
staff
  importance of 10–11
  quality of 17–18, 24, 83–4, 91–3, 95–8